Run That by Me Again

Run That by Me Again

Selected Essays from "Absolutes" to the "Things That Can Be Otherwise"

JAMES V. SCHALL, SJ

TAN Books
Charlotte, North Carolina

Cover design by Caroline K. Green

Cover image: Spiral Staircase © martinho Smart/Shutterstock

Library of Congress Control Number: 2018950326

ISBN: 978-1-5051-1133-0

Published in the United States by
TAN Books
PO Box 410487
Charlotte, NC 28241
www.TANBooks.com

Printed in the United States of America

"We heard with our own ears, O God, our fathers have told us the story of the things you did in their days, you yourself, in days long ago."

—Psalm 44:1–2

"If we would say that man is too insignificant to deserve communion with God, we must indeed be very great to judge."

—Pascal, *Pensées*, no. 511

"Middling people are shocked at the wickedness of the wicked. Gibbie, who knew both so well, was shocked only at the wickedness of the righteous. He never came quite to understand Mr. Schlater; the inconsistent never can be understood. That only which has absolute reason in it can be understood of man. There is a bewilderment about the very nature of evil which only He who made us capable of evil that we might be good, can comprehend."

—George MacDonald, *Sir Gibbie*, in
George MacDonald: An Anthology, no. 326

"'Then the prophecies of the old songs turned out to be true, after a fashion,' said Bilbo. 'Of course,' said Gandalf. 'And why should they not prove true? Surely you don't disbelieve the prophecies, because you had a hand in bringing them about yourself? You don't really suppose, do you, that all your adventures and escapes were

*managed by mere luck, just for your sole benefit? You are
a very fine person, Mr. Baggins, and I am very fond of you;
but you are only quite a little fellow in a wide world, after
all.' 'Thank goodness,' said Bilbo laughing, and handed
him the tobacco-jar."*

—J. R. R. Tolkien, Last lines in *The Hobbit*

*"Truth consists in the equation of intellect and thing. . . .
Now the intellect that is the cause of the thing is related to
it as its rule and measure; whereas the converse is the case
with the intellect that receives its knowledge from things.
When, therefore, things are the measure and rule of the
intellect, truth consists in the equation of the intellect to the
thing; as happens in ourselves. For according as a thing
is, or is not, our thoughts or our words about it are true
or false. But when the intellect is the rule or measure of
things, truth consists in the equation of things to intellect;
just as the work of an artist is said to be true when it is in
accordance with his art."*

—Thomas Aquinas, *Summa Theologiae*, I, 21, 2

*"A philosopher has of necessity tasted the other pleasures
since childhood, but it isn't necessary for a profit-lover to
taste or experience the pleasure of learning the nature of
the things that are and how sweet it is. Indeed, even if he
were eager to taste it, he couldn't easily do so."*

—Plato, *The Republic*, IX, 582b

CONTENTS

ACKNOWLEDGMENTS

THE author wishes to thank the editors of the following sites and sources for permission to reprint material of the author that was previously published.

From *The Catholic Thing*, chapters 1–4, 7, 9–11, 14, 16, 19–22, 24, 30–32, 35, 37, 39–41, 43, 45–46, 49–51, 53.

From the *Catholic World Report*, chapters 12–13, 25.

From the *University Bookman*, chapters 5–6, 26, 38, 42, 48, 54.

From *The Hill*, chapters 8, 23, 27, 47, 52.

From *Gilbert Magazine*, chapter 28, 44.

From *Crisis Magazine*, chapters 29, 36,

From *MercatorNet*, chapters 33–34, 55.

From aleteia.org, chapters 17–18.

PREFACE

THE title of this collection of essays, *Run That by Me Again*, is a colloquialism that comes from a common experience that we all have probably had at one time or another. We hear something that is presented or explained to us that does not quite make sense. After a bit, the speaker is waiting for our reaction to his wisdom. We, frankly, do not want to admit that we understood very little of the whole gist or argument. So we request that the narrator "run" what he said by us one more time. And often it works. We really do need to hear many things more than once to see the full force of their initial statement. Once understood, we can better state why we agree or disagree with what we have heard and on what basis.

This book is a collection of some fifty-five sundry essays, each relatively brief. They cover a wide range of related and unrelated topics. One of the glories of a book of selected essays is that most anything can come up. In this world, we can find no real limit of interesting things to consider. While few readers will have read any of these particular essays previously, still most of the topics treated are ones that are in common circulation and interest. Most people have given some attention to evil, libraries, war, and even to "cocktail time" and the meaning of Easter. In that sense, each of these essays can be imagined as taking a second or third look at issues that we all need to or would like to think about again and again. And I suppose some of these essays are on topics that we do not want to think about but we know that we should.

We are not beings who understand what we learn once and for all. We will often find that things look quite different at fifty than they did when we were twenty. By our eighties, we barely recollect what we maintained when we were in our teens. And yet we are quite conscious that we are the same person that we were in all the stages of growth in our lives. We are given one life to lead and we are leading it, seeking to understand it. We realize that the responsibility for many things that now exist in the world, whether we like it or not, resides in us, in our actions and choices.

A book of collected essays, I think, has certain advantages. Many of these essays are on topics that are obviously related to each other. Determinism and absolutes, for example, have something to do with each other. The future and outer space touch on each other. Still, each separate topic retains its own intelligibility. Likewise, we seldom see put together side by side theological, literary, and philosophic topics. The essays in this book do not follow any chronological or logical order. There is reason for this. It keeps before us the uniqueness of each topic as it comes up. Just as in life, we never know what sort of issue will turn up that we must deal with next.

But when we reread something, when we let our minds run through a known issue again, we realize the attention that we have to give to things if we are to understand them. And I would add that, strictly speaking, we cannot understand absolutely everything about any real thing, including its existence. No doubt our own talents, or lack thereof, have something to do with what we learn from our experience. Some people probably can go through something twenty times and never get it; others get it the first time through. Still others understand it well enough but do not want to admit the truth of something. Such an admission would interfere with the way they live. Given a choice, truth was sacrificed to custom or desire.

These essays were all written during the last decade, a decade that saw an astonishingly rapid secularization of public life, many aspects of which are noted in these chapters. However, the more recent changes in the Supreme Court, the isolation of ISIS, and the increased awareness of the worth of a nation-state have caused their own reactions. Any welcome change back to a constitutional and sensible public life is resisted. We have here another indication that changes can be unexpected and occur in the places where we never would expect them. When we take a second look and run back over things we thought most likely to happen, we find that they did not, or at least not in the way we expected. We have to run our minds over the fact that what we were sure would happen turned out differently, sometimes for the worse but also sometimes for the better.

At the beginning of this book, the reader will find six quotations—one from a Psalm, one from Pascal, others from George MacDonald, J. R. R. Tolkien, Thomas Aquinas, and finally Plato. I will return to these initial readings in the conclusion of this book. But I would prefer that the book not be read till each of the quotations is read and thought over for a bit. The spirit of much of what I have written in these selected essays is found in one or other of these short readings. As Robert Sokolowski said in his excellent book *Pictures, Quotations, and Distinctions*, the mere fact that we can cite what someone else has said before us and put it in our own context is a rare privilege.[1] The citations give some sense of those with whom we would like to associate ourselves in the things that count. They also speak through us to others who would otherwise probably never have heard of these written words. Thus, when they run by me again, they run through the minds of others for the first time.

The essay, as I have often said, is a favorite literary form of mine. My life has been greatly expanded because Belloc told us in short essays, often selected and collected, of where he walked or sailed, of what he read. The essay does not replace the book or the treatise, let alone the symphony, the novel, or the painting. Our lives are not filled solely with either-ors but with both-ands. As I say in the second essay, the most astonishing thing about this world is its abundance. By letting these essays "run by us" again, we can, hopefully, catch some of the variety and richness of the world *that is*. The times and places of our lives lead us to the times and places of any lives in any time and place.

Many essays in this collection, like many essays on the classical tradition itself, begin with the proposition "on," as if to say that we would like to spend some time and attention "on" all the things *that are*. Indeed, I think that this pausing to dwell "on" any one thing or on all things is what the essay makes easily available to us. It is not everything,

---

[1]   Robert Sokolowski, *Pictures, Quotations, and Distinctions* (Notre Dame: University of Notre Dame Press, 1992).

but like creation itself, it has something to do with a "beginning." And anything that has to do with a beginning, sooner or later, has something to do with an ending. These are some of the things that will, hopefully, be found by running these things by us again.

CHAPTER 1

ON ABSOLUTES

THE past participle of the Latin verb *absolvere* is *absolutus*. It means "freed from any restrictions." Modern man wants no "absolutes." He wants to be loosed from things binding for all times and places. An "absolute" refers to lines not to be crossed. *Moral* absolutes, however, can be crossed. Of course "thou shalt not kill" does not mean that no killings will take place. It means that, if crossed, "absolute" consequences, either in the here or hereafter, will follow. All things not forgiven remain with us. Indeed, they remain with us even if they are forgiven. Our deeds and words form the character into which we have made ourselves. We are always a "this someone" who, in the days of our mortality, did or did not do this or that.

It is easy to imagine why we might want to rid the world of absolutes. Their elimination would, presumably, free us to do whatever we wanted to do with no fear of untoward repercussions. But let us suppose that we want to deny the existence of absolutes; how would we go about doing so?

No doubt, if I want to eliminate the prohibition against murder or stealing, I want it removed only for my own case. I do not want it universalized. I do not want others to feel perfectly free to wipe me out or, with impunity, to abscond unscathed with my hard-earned goods. We cannot

1

have it both ways. So, viewed from this angle, we really do not want absolutes abolished except as convenient for ourselves.

But if we still insist on abolishing absolutes, we might approach the issue from the angle of authority. Who says that any absolutes exist? Scripture, for instance, has a couple or pretty hefty "thou shalt nots." But why should we bother about Scripture? Who knows what was actually said? Who was around to check the accuracy of its recorded prohibitions? Even then, perhaps the "thou shalt nots" held only in that ancient time or in those strange customs.

Someone like Descartes even worried that maybe the devil was deceiving us so that we could not rely on our senses to tell us anything reliable about what is going on in the world. But if no God exists, or if we cannot figure out who said what, it is senseless to trust any authority that sets down absolutes. When Christ pardoned the lady caught in adultery, he told her, "Go and sin no more." Wasn't he violating her "rights" to live the way she wanted to live?

Still, if we find no divine authority capable of defining or enforcing absolutes, what about the state? Can't it enforce whatever it wants? Isn't that what Hobbes taught? Civil authority seems to be pretty much absolute. But states differ. They can change from day to day what they consider absolute. Opposites can be absolutes on given days.

Likewise, scientifically inter-related absolutes seem to exist. If they did not hold, the world would not stay together. No one wants to change the speed of light or the fact that we human beings are born with hands and brains. The range of sound waves that we can and cannot hear seems pretty absolute.

When we come right down to it, the number of absolutes that we might want to change are few. The only way an outfielder can catch a fly ball is if a) the ball is not made of lead, b) a batter hits the fly, c) the ball comes down on an arc, and d) the legs, eyes, and hand of the fielder are so coordinated that they are there where the ball comes down. If these absolutes are not permanent, don't bother to take me out to the ball game.

If the world were not full of absolutes, we could not live in it. Indeed, we would not want to live in it. The problem that we human beings have concerns only a few absolutes. These are the absolutes that indicate what we are and how we ought to live, even when we do not observe them.

The annoying trouble with absolutes usually shows up when we do not observe them. For some reason, all sorts of unwelcome things happen to ourselves or others that we are reluctant to attribute to the absolutes. We develop a whole rhetoric that usually ends up reassuring us that what we did was just fine. The fact is that no one can violate any absolute without trying to give some reason why it is quite all right.

Where does this leave us? We usually end up proving the existence of absolutes by seeing that our reasons to prove them wrong actually prove them right. The witticism that no good deed goes unpunished deserves one addendum: "No bad deed," as Plato said, "goes unpunished either." That too is an absolute.

CHAPTER 2

ON ABUNDANCE

THE dominant contemporary "feeling" is that we live in a parsimonious world. Nature is running out of gas. Natural resources are scandalously "used up," never to be replaced. Besides, too many people exist on the planet consuming everything in sight. Species of birds and bugs die out. "Consumerism" knows no bounds. The great enemy of mankind is man himself. He is out of control. Survival prospects for even a small number of gaunt human beings are grim. We must act now, decisively, before it is too late.

This doomsday scenario is found in schools, media, governments, churches, and businesses. In the minds of its advocates, its validity is stronger than any faith. To question its tenets approaches blasphemy. Mother Earth is finally unveiled as a vengeful goddess. Many find meaning in this collective panic over presumed decreasing resources. It provides an urgent mission. We can now venture forth in a mighty cause to save the world from itself. Evil is now defined not by sins but by our greedy use of spare resources. Governments are empowered with the welcome task of controlling man by drastically limiting the goods needed for his long-term survival down the planetary ages.

Is there an alternate vision? Why does not the evidence incline us to look at the world's extraordinary abundance? How is it possible that already so much was available to us for so long? The word *abundance* means overflow, plenty. It comes from the Latin word for wave (*unda*). When a wave crashes over itself, the sea is filled, full, surging with overflowing waters. The more puzzling thing about the world is not that it contains too little for its purposes, but, astonishingly, way too much, as if it had another purpose in mind.

The initial question is not: "How many resources do we have?" But, "Do we have sufficient and more than sufficient resources for the purpose of our existence on this earth?" Calculations about what might be needed and what is given have little direct relation to the reason why man exists on this planet. No reason can be found to think that, when man ends his stay on this planet, resources to support him will have run out at the same time

Panic about sufficient resources usually arises from the assumption that members of the human race are to remain on this planet for as long as the planet survives. The projections of scarcity are based on this doubtful premise. The destiny and purpose of humanity on this planet are not primarily geared to keeping a few of its billions of members alive down the course of time. Almost all ecology theories about resources and man are premised on the dubious supposition that man has only a this-worldly purpose for his existence. Thus keeping some of the race alive for as long as possible becomes man's only intelligible end.

The second presumption of the scarcity syndrome is that human beings do not have brains, or, at least, brains that can deal with their problems as they arise. When I use the word *abundance* to describe what is available to us, I include the human mind's capacity to learn both what is actually there in reality and how it might be used. We do not know what kinds of technology will be available to us in a century or two. If we predicted the twentieth century based on what men knew in the year 1900, it would never have included the computer, space exploration, or plant research. It is no accident that a hostile relation exists between the limits to growth school and science/technology.

If we approach our lot on this earth from the viewpoint of abundance, we will see that the availability of resources is itself a function of our knowledge plus the enormous riches that are already found on this planet. Nature and mind are not simply the result of some accident. With mind and nature, we are given much material abundance to fulfill the purpose for which we are created. This purpose is not for some few members of the human race to be alive when the earth finally burns out, or only to transport themselves to some other planet and continue on *ad infinitum*.

The purpose of the human race, itself also part of nature, is that each of the finite numbers that God had created is free to reach or reject his transcendent end. The earth is man's dominion wherein he is to achieve an end that is not simply keeping the planet garden-like. But the caring for the earth is a sidelight to caring for one's own soul and those of others. Revelation is clear that our inner-worldly end will come when God chooses, when we least expect it, not when we run out of abundant resources.

CHAPTER 3

ON THE WHOLE HUMAN RACE

THE word *man* (*homo*, in Latin, with equivalent words in most languages) is the name we give in English to an abstract concept designed intelligibly to include every existing human being who ever lived, could live, or will live. It states what they have in common and what distinguishes them from other beings. It does not deny that each person who ever lived is embodied in a way that distinguishes and separates him from everyone else who ever lived.

Individual persons cannot be predicated of each other. I cannot say Tom is John, but I can say John is a man; Tom is a man. Here, by "man," we do not mean "male" (*vir*), which is also a valid abstract concept that, like female, designates and distinguishes many individuals of the same kind. The mind is luminous, flexible. It can understand different meanings to the same words or many words in different languages for the same concept. Learning properly to distinguish and remember is what intelligence and education are all about. Intelligence is what makes us more than ourselves, makes us able to know what is not ourselves.

If there were a race of rational beings on some planet in a distant galaxy, would we include them? Probably. What about every human being conceived (note the word) on this planet from the first appearance of man? Yes, it would include them all. What if this human race set up a camp on Mars or some other non-earthly spot and it succeeded to continue there, would it include them? No problem.

The human race, as such, does not include the gods or the animals, even though these may exist in abundance and be necessary for continued human existence. If some asteroid crashed into our Earth to destroy it, would that be the end of the human race if none of this species had managed to exist elsewhere? Yes, probably. But the concept of what-it-is-to-be-a-human being would remain the same if any mind to think it existed. We hear talk of a race of clones or hybrids of animal and man. These are things that we may possibly bring forth although, in fact, we ought to have sense enough not to do so.

Does "the whole human race" have a purpose other than as intelligible? No, only individual human beings have "purposes." The concept "man," however, does enable us to think of our lot, to think about what we all are. The "whole human race" does not exist in one time or in one place. It exists sequentially and scattered across the planet and in different eras.

This race speaks some seven thousand different languages, which themselves come and go, change. If men come across a language they do not know, they figure out what it is saying. Generally speaking, all languages can be made intelligible to all other languages. This capacity implies that human beings have some capacity to live together, to understand each other, however difficult it may be for an Englishman to speak Mandarin or Zulu. Translating one language into another is a major industry. And yes, we miss a lot in translation.

We see estimates that, thus far, something over a hundred billion people were born on this Earth. Some seven billion are still alive. The population of the dead thus is huge. How many remain yet to be born? Many modern ecological theories claim roughly to know this figure by extrapolating on existing resource availability. Much doomsday speculation lies in such theories combined with bad economics and bad science. It is highly doubtful that the human race exists for no purpose. If we begin with the theological premise that each conceived person is created for eternal life, we conclude that the human race exists so that each person reaches this transcendent end. It can only be reached through death. Aquinas held that the number of human beings intended to exist was finite. This limit means that the actual race is not intended just to go on and on in this world.

So the primary purpose of the human race is not simply to keep itself going in time and space for as long as possible. The purpose of the human race is not separable from the purpose of each of its individual members. That is, the end includes a personal eternal life within a "city" that includes God and other beings likewise made for this end.

This end, however, has to be individually chosen. Unless it can be rejected, it would not be worth having, for it would not be freely accepted. How does one go about rejecting it? By choosing not to observe the commandments. You're kidding? Nope, dead serious. Such is the drama of the whole human race.

CHAPTER 4

ON BLASPHEMY

CHRIST was often accused of blasphemy. Usually, the accusation occurred when he performed a miracle, say, on a Sabbath. Christ never condemned the Jewish laws against blasphemy. What he did rather was, by his works, to show that he was God. He did not mock Yahweh. He did not blaspheme his Father. He and the Father were one.

Christ was executed according to the Roman Law, by crucifixion, not Jewish Law, by stoning. The effective charge was blasphemy, the claim that he was God. His crucifixion was justified by the blasphemy charges. The Romans, who cared little for Jewish quibbles, decided to overlook validity of these accusations.

What appears in the news almost daily are alleged violations of Muslim laws against blasphemy. To "insult" or "mock" Allah, Mohammed, or the *Qur'an* is said to merit death. It does not matter under what civil jurisdiction the presumed blasphemy occurs—in Saudi Arabia, Amsterdam, Syria, Pakistan, Paris, or wherever. Every Muslim is somehow designated to enforce the law. It claims universal jurisdiction.

Western "hate-speech" laws are a secular version of blasphemy laws, only what we cannot talk about is not God but certain men or issues. Laws of calumny, libel, or slander mean that we are required to speak the truth about

God and man. Free speech and free press, however, also belong to blasphemy considerations. Finding the truth of some accusation or claim is not always easy. Some things should be ridiculed. The classic word is "tolerate" possible errors. The people who least want to be investigated are sometimes those who should be investigated. To deny the existence of God or Allah is not blasphemy. Blasphemy laws remain, apparently, even if there is no God or Allah. What causes the problem is not the blasphemy itself but the dangerous way people react to it. Several writers have mentioned that *Charlie Hebdo* also mocked Christ and the pope, not just Allah and Mohammed. The difference was that no Christian thought it all right, on that basis, to shoot anyone. Many Muslims evidently do not see it that way. It is the crossing of that line where the problem lies with Islam.

The notion of limits to free speech is ancient. Aristotle said that if our wit hurts others, it should be moderated. On the other hand, an obligation also exists to the truth. It is one thing to ridicule something that is true, another something false and dangerous. If nothing can be mocked, everything is "true." Few had problems with mocking Hitler, Stalin, or Khomeini. We can be so sensitive that we cannot say anything about anyone. The whole industry of political cartoons and satire is a noble one. Never to have a cartoon prodding us is a sign of indifference to what we are about.

I think that the current anti-hate laws are very dangerous. In the case of Islam, they prevent an honest discussion of what Islam is about. Such laws allow a government to define what can and cannot be freely and properly discussed. Anti-racism, anti-gay, and anti-feminist laws fall into this category.

On the other hand, we find a general silence about murders of Christians. Our government and media in the recent past seem to have a policy of seldom mentioning any relation between "terrorists" and Islam. Yet they never really acknowledge in any detail that Christians are killed by Muslims. Few people even know the extent of today's Christian martyrdom.

In an Interview in *Le Figaro,* Rémi Brague pointed out that, when it comes to abortion, we insist on calling it something else, a "procedure" or "aiding health of the mother." The "what is aborted" is never a "human person," which it is. So we lie. Our laws and speech customs go along with the lies.

In their own minds, the Muslim "terrorists" are not terrorists. They are defenders of Allah. The problem their action against blasphemy brings up is specific. It was pinpointed by Benedict XVI. Is it ever permitted to kill in the name of Allah? If it is, and it seems to be, we are dealing with something well beyond "blasphemy" and its laws.

Briefly, if we have a religion that says its god approves killing for any statement of ridicule of its position, we have to conclude that this god cannot be god. Further, we have to acknowledge that riots that arise to defend this position are outside the pale of civilization.

The principle of respecting all religions has a limit. That limit is: "What does the religion hold?" If it holds it to be all right to kill blasphemers, it cannot be a true religion. This is not to approve unrestricted mockery. It is to point out that if we remove these blasphemy laws and sanctions from Islam as violating some standard besides the "will" of Allah, it would not still be historical Islam.

CHAPTER 5

"ET TU, BRUTE?"

CAESAR was killed on the famous "Ides" of March 44 BC. The murder took place in the Senate, then meeting in the Theater of Pompey. Caesar had acquired dictatorial powers. Technically, the office of "dictator" was a legal one. It was not as such illegitimate. It was designed for times of emergency to allow firm leadership that was not hampered by divisions of authority between the two consuls and the tribunate which ruled in times of peace. Brutus, Cassius, and others interpreted this act as a step toward permanent dictatorship. Thus, opposition to tyranny was the stated motive for their participation in the killing of Caesar. The dictatorial office itself was legally supposed to last for six months and therefore was limited by time and not simply absolute.

Caesar was said to have been stabbed twenty-three times, only one of which was said by a doctor to have been fatal. By so doing, each of the conspirators showed his agreement with the act of killing Caesar. The drama of his death has always fascinated and educated anyone who heard of it. We know it mostly in its most elegant form through Shakespeare's play. Whether it was Caesar or his killers who were the nobler is an abidingly controverted question, one worth meditation in any liberal education. Some sense can be made of either position.

The famous line "*Et tu, Brute*—and you too Brutus" was probably never spoken by Caesar. In Shakespeare, the words are fundamental to understanding the depths of the drama. Most ancient historians say that Caesar was silent at his death, though others say that he uttered a Greek phrase that meant much the same, "And you, also, young man?" In any case, he did not anticipate the plot against his life by men whom he considered friends and fellow senators.

Two things are to be noted about Caesar's death. First, when meeting in the Senate, everyone was supposed to be unarmed. Roman legions entered the city unarmed to signify that it was ruled by law, not force. When the first man stabbed Caesar in the plot, Caesar is said to have uttered, astonished, "But this is violence!" Proceedings in the Senate were by speech, not arms. Caesar was obeying this senatorial law; the conspirators were not. From this point of view, Caesar was the more noble man.

Secondly, Brutus and Caesar were friends. The drama of Shakespeare is sometimes thought to be really the drama of Brutus, not Caesar. It was tyrants who were said to have no friends. Because of their bonds of loyalty, friends were said to be more dangerous to tyrants than separate individuals. In this setting, Brutus broke his friendship with Caesar because Caesar became a tyrant in his view.

The classic question is the relation of duty to friend and duty to country or to God. Whether Caesar was the sort of tyrant that Brutus pictured him to be might be questioned. Caesar was an accomplished man. And the morality of Brutus's deed hinges on this estimate of tyranny, together with the legitimacy of tyrannicide in general. Brutus, along with Cicero, did maintain that the killing of a tyrant was an act of courage for the good of the country.

Allan Bloom, in his discussion of this play (*Shakespeare's Politics*), calls Caesar a "mortal God." That is, Caesar was someone who had so many talents and qualities that he rose above everyone else. He had the title to rule that comes from an excellence that makes everyone better. The Greeks said of such a man that a polity, when he rarely happens along, has two choices: either exile him or make him king lest he corrupt the polity.

But I happened to come across a copy of Mark Anthony's brief funeral oration for Caesar. It is a remarkable example of rhetoric. I want to reflect on Anthony's view of Brutus. Ironically, in subsequent history, Brutus came to stand for liberty, while Caesar stood for tyranny and power. Anthony was an admirer of Caesar and himself an eloquent man. He understood that what was at stake was the reputation of Caesar down the ages.

On reading these accounts, we begin to suspect that something good can be said of the worst of men, and something dubious of the best. Anthony famously begins: "Friends, Romans and country, lend me your ear. I have come to bury Caesar, not to praise him." Yet Anthony's "burial" ends in the highest praise of Caesar. This affirmation is just the opposite of what we might expect. Anthony does not attack Brutus directly, although it is clear that he loathes him and his deed. What he does is to examine the basis of Brutus's judgment about Caesar.

Brutus was a fine and noble man. He stood for the best of classical Roman virtues. He thought he was displaying them in deciding to participate in the plot against Caesar, his friend and fellow senator. People would rely on Brutus's reputation to decide which view was right. Anthony's task thus was to defend Caesar by making Brutus out to be vain and self-serving.

The good that a man does goes with him to the grave. It is his evil deeds that live on. If we think of all the eulogies we have ever heard, the opposite almost seems the norm. *De mortuis, nil nisi bonum*, as the old saying went. "Of the dead, we say only the good things." Brutus had tried to portray Caesar as an evil tyrant. What was the basis of the accusation?

Anthony's task then was to take Brutus's reputation down a peg. He lists the things that "the noble Brutus" used to prove his point. Caesar was "ambitious." Anthony admits that "were it so" it was a "grievous fault." But was it so? Caesar certainly paid for it by Brutus's hand if he had that fault. "But Brutus is an honorable man"—so, as such, his testimony must be true.

Anthony affirms that Caesar was his own friend, "faithful and just" to him. But Brutus sees it otherwise. Caesar brought many captives home. Their ransoms brought in much wealth for others. Anthony wondered: Was this "ambitious" for himself?

Appealing to the poor is an ancient custom. When the poor entreat Caesar, was this a sign of ambition when Caesar "wept" over them? "Ambition," Anthony observes, if it exists, should be made of "sterner" stuff. But Brutus, the "honorable" man, says otherwise.

Anthony recalls that during the Lupeacalia festivities he offered the crown to Caesar three times. Three tines he refused it. But Brutus said he was "ambitious." Anthony tells us that he is not speaking to "disprove" Brutus's accusations but only of what he knew. People loved Caesar not without reason.

Anthony leaves it at that. Brutus is an "honorable" man the refrain continues. But obviously, Anthony thinks that Brutus has no real proof of his accusation that Caesar was "ambitious," that he would actually become what Brutus feared.

Anthony's last words are of despair, or perhaps transcendence. Judgment has fled to the beasts. Plato in the same situation placed it with the gods. Anthony concludes: "Men have lost their reason." I cannot but think that the effect of Anthony's speech on most of us is rather that it was precisely in its being lost, that reason could be again found in our souls.

CHAPTER 6

THE ROAD TO "REUNION" EXAMINED

O N the front page of *L'Osservatore Romano*, English, for November 4, 2016, we find two headlines occasioned by the Holy Father's trip to Sweden on the five hundredth anniversary of the Reformation. One headline reads "On the Path toward Full Communion" while the second one reads "Changing History."

I probably would not have paid much attention to these headlines were it not for the fact that a neighbor had just given me a photocopy of Msgr. Ronald Knox's famous satirical essay "Reunion All Round," an essay found in his 1928 Sheed & Ward book *Essays in Satire*. Even back in ancient times like 1928, we find rumblings about the reunification of the Christian churches and other religions into what has come to be called in our time "The World Parliament of Religion." World government, it seems, prefers to have these myriads of religious fanatics under one management roof. All believers, no matter what they maintain, should come together in a spirit of brotherly love to solve the world's problems, which, to tell the truth, are mostly caused, according to their critics, by their stubborn and insignificant differences.

Knox's essay is most amusing. The text is printed in that old Germanic script that the letter *s*, as in "s" prints *f*, with *ct* joined by a curve from the *c* to the *t*. The essay, in fact, is filled with theology, canon law, liturgical practices, and the history of religion. Right away, we catch the flavor of the proposal from the initial dedication: "Being a Plea for the Inclufion within the *Church of England* of all *Mahometans, Jews, Buddhifts,* fubmitted to the confideration of the British Public." Definitely, this is a "modest," refined proposal, on the model of Swift.

At first sight, of course, the differences in religious belief and practice appear insurmountable. Things like marriage customs and metaphysical perceptions hamper the way. But this proposal comes from that "liberal mind" that sees all things happily reconcilable with proper attention to compromise, compassion, and, yes, contradiction.

Openness to everything is the key operative concept in resolving all ecclesial difficulties. "There is no progress in Humanity," we read, "without the surmounting of Obstacles; thus we are now all agree'd that *Satan*, far from meaning any harm to our Race when he brought Sin into the World, was most excellently dispos'd toward us. . . ." Needless to emphasize, this rendering Satan benevolent is a definite advance in theological thinking. It has been too long since anyone has put a good word in for Satan.

What was Satan up to, then? He did not want the human race "languishing" in that state of innocent bliss in which the poor angels found themselves bored to death. He wanted to put a little "excitement" into our lives. So we can all now agree to set aside this slander too often perpetrated by the preachers against the Angel of Light that Lucifer was.

With this understanding that the causes given for divisions within Christendom are all illusory, a new future seems open. "I conceive, then, that within a few years of the present Date (1928), the Division of Christians into Sects for purposes of Worship will have utterly disappeared, and we shall find one great United Protestant Church extending throughout the civilized World." Even though we are now some ninety years away from this pioneering endeavor, we see, as I intimated, signs that its spirit is not wholly dead.

With confidence in progress, we may still find problems with odd branches like the Seventh Day Adventists. They demand that Saturday be a day of rest. The solution is easy. Make both Saturday and Sunday days of rest. We thus have "two days instead of one in every seven in which we can lie abed till Noon, overeat ourselves, go out driving in the Country, and dine away from home under the colour of sparing trouble to our Domesticks." We have here both an eminently practical solution and an unexpected view of the status of Sabbath spiritual activities of the faithful on the days of rest throughout the Empire.

The Orthodox, then as now, seem to present a special problem for the unifiers. This "*Filioque* (controversy about the Creed) will clearly have to disappear." Since the Creed is made up of reactions to differing heresies, most of which still need reconciling, the solution would be for a communal recitation of the Creed in which one only says that part with which he agrees. The Russian solution, which could be assigned also to the Sultan of Turkey, of letting state power decide doctrine seems likewise possible.

But a further problem arises with the Orthodox; namely, their liturgy, in which fireworks are set off at New Year's. The Orthodox are hundreds of years out-of-date with their ancient language, their "Mumblings, Bobbings, Bowings,

Shutting and Opening of Doors, Kissings, Gesticulatings, etc." Also all icons need to be lifted high on church walls so that "nobody will worship them."

In the treatment of what to do about Muslims, the reform proposal was clearly way ahead of its time. We see the same problems today, after the 2016 Muslin invasion of Europe (often, erroneously, called immigration), that were envisioned in this unification proposal. We definitely cannot any longer call Mohammed a "false Prophet." His only real quarrel with the Christian sects was over "Mariolatry and some unduly strict views they held about marriage." Again this controversy could be solved. The Muslim practice of four wives and the Christian practice of one could split the difference, with each having two. This would solve the problem that the Muslims had with the supply of enough women to meet the demand of four to each man.

This compromise, this reliance on mathematics to solve irreconcilable issues, applies to another area of Muslim and Christian differences. "We shall, of course, adopt at the same time the Mahometan Rule, by which a man may at any time turn his Wife out of doors, upon finding her displeasing to himself, and take a new one, modifying it only so far, as to extend the Privilege equally with the Wife, so as to the Husband." This solution seems quite reasonable.

Another issue came up about liturgical practices. The Muslims like to chant from their Sacred Book. So some compromise could be worked out in the First Reading in the Christian liturgy. "Since we have nowadays so little use for the *Old Testament*, Readings from the *Coran* should be substituted for it in the Divine Service."

Lest we think this approach might lead to some problem, we have the following rationale which follows some of the recent discussions about a German critical edition of the Qur'an:

> If any man object that this [reading of the Coran at Liturgy] might lead to a superstitious Belief in the Facts therein alleged'd, I would point out for his Comfort that in a very short Time the Critical Study will come to be expended on the latter Book [*Coran*], which has hitherto investigated the former (the Old Testament), with such happy Results; and consequently within twenty years' time we should be in no more danger of giving Credit to the Miracles of Mahomet, than we are in now of stomaching the *History of Joshua*.

Some attention is given to the noisy Muslim custom of calling to prayer versus church bells as well as to the direction we face while praying. The Muslims face Mecca while the Westerners face Chicago. Each should be given a compass so when the call to prayer comes, the believer can face whatever direction he wants knowing where the magnetic pole is located.

On another contemporary note, mindful of the pleas for dialogue, we recall the fact that "there are the [Muslim] Assassins, who hold it to be just and lawful to kill a man in virtue of a Disagreement about Religion, and did lately murder a man very horribly in the city of Paris." The advice here, however, is not to treat these killers as public Enemies, but "as erring Brethren."

The assassins should be admitted into the community. And we should preach to them from our sacred books. They will see that such killing gives rise to "blood-feuds" and its widespread practice makes the "Tenure of Life" for all of us less secure. When we reason with these violent gentlemen in this pious way, "doubtless in a very short time they would have learned to take a more lenient view of doctrinal Irregularities."

But the Muslims are not the only ones needing reconciliation. Most of the early heresies came out of the notion that matter is evil. Such a doctrine is simply unheard of by the "Thinkers of our Time." It seems that "Enlightened People like ourselves" are more interested in things that we do "with Fists, Feet, and Muscles . . . than any activity of the Brains." If matter were evil, we would not "seek bodily Health by every possible means." The way to avoid this evil Manichean thesis is to recognize that all the bad things are "necessary evils" and thus have no moral import for us.

Whether the Church of Rome can be accommodated is a special problem. "I know we are commonly told, That this will never be achiev'd, by Reason of Extreme Obstinacy and Perversity of this Sect." This Roman stubbornness is based on numbers. When the Papists see their numbers declining, they will become more flexible. Science helps us. We know now "that all Survival in the World is *a Survival of the Fittest*, and that two Instincts chiefly make an Organization fit to survive, namely *the Will to Live* and the Desire to propagate its kind." The Roman cult of Martyrs and Celibacy should soon take care of this problem. The then noted increase of Catholic numbers was not due principally to conversions but to the immigration of the Irish. These prolific folks at the time were busy "stocking five Continents with Papists."

To halt this danger, it was proposed at the time (shades of the future abortion industry and one-child Chinese law) that "we should make it a criminal Offense for the future, that any Papist should be allowed to marry, or have Issue: the Offense itself to be punished with Death, and the resulting Issue to be expos'd on some Hill-side, lest it should grow up infected with the gross Superstition of its Parents." If we look today back on the present condition of the Papists in Ireland, we can see that this worry of an Irish take-over of the world was grossly exaggerated.

In this coming unified world religion, the only doctrinal issue would be required. Everyone is to take a "Declaration of Loyalty to the Church." "It would be an Affirmation of a general Dissent from the Doctrines contain'd in the *Thirty-Nine Articles of Religion.*" Surely anyone could agree to make such a "dissent": "I firmly dissent from any doctrinal statement."

What to do about the pope and the cardinals? "The Pope himself I would allow to take the rank of a retired Military Bishop, thus leaving him with the Insignia of Power, without any Sphere in which to exercise it." And "the Cardinals I would disperse among the Common-rooms of Oxford and Cambridge where they could exercise their Talent for Intrigue without having any serious effect."

Finally we come to the Atheists. They present a lesser problem than the religionists who differ on all sorts of minor inherited doctrine and practice. The Atheists have "only one single Quarrel to patch up, namely, as to whether any God exists, or not." All we need to do is to "ease" their "conscience on this single matter." They have no real reliance to any inherited view of what to profess.

If we could get our theologians to agree that God is both "Existent and Non-Existent," then we could each affirm with confidence our position without hurt to the other view. With this marvelously illuminating approach, we can all live together and profess a common Creed. We can "recognize the Divine Governor of the Universe as One who exists, yet does not exist, causes Sin, yet hates it, yet does not punish it, and promises us in Heaven a Happiness, in which we shall not have any Consciousness to enjoy." This solution, no doubt, is the perfect resolution of the famous controversy between negative and positive theology about whether we best affirm what God is or what he is not.

The concluding exhortation is admirable. It could in fact have been written by the present justices of the Supreme Court, or by the philosophical faculty of most any expensive university in the world. It reads: "Thank God in these days of Enlightenment and Establishment, everyone has a right to his own Opinions, and chiefly to the Opinion, That nobody else has a right to their's. It shall go hard, but within a century at most we shall make the *Church of England* true to her Catholic vocation, which is, plainly, to include within her Borders every possible Shade of Belief."

On finishing such an inspiring treatise, we can perhaps wonder whether the satirical essay is not, in fact, a form of prophecy.

CHAPTER 7

ON CREATION

W E talk about creation, about "caring" for the earth for future generations, about "abusing" it. How do we think about these things? We stand at a great divide: either the cosmos was deliberately created as a willed order or it was always there. It just happened along.

Biblical information about creation tells us that it is "good," that it fits together, and that it bespeaks the glory of God. It is not itself a "god," nor is God part of it. The cosmos was made for man, not the other way around. Each human individual has a purpose that transcends the cosmos itself and connects him with its origin. The main concern is with the final destiny of each member of the human species. Each person is judged for what he freely did during his allotted lifetime, whenever, wherever, or whatever it was, great or small.

Included in creation are its natural riches, plus human brains and hands. The abundance of creation was evidently provided so that through it, human beings could achieve their purpose. Man's intelligence gave him "dominion" over other creatures and goods found already present in this creation. Their perfection is related to his.

Man is a late-arriving creature within the cosmos. He has expanded his planetary numbers fairly rapidly to something over seven billion. The reason he could sustain these numbers was because he learned how to harness the good things found already there for his needs on this earth.

Even a century ago, we had little idea about how richly this planet was endowed. Population increases are looked at either as threats or as blessings. Some maintain that we are rapidly running out of resources. We must reduce and control our numbers to last down the ages. Others maintain that we can provide for ourselves if we will. What we are given, what we are, and what our purpose is; these issues are related to each other.

Behind these diverse assumptions looms the question of what the earth is for in the light of what human beings are for. We hear much talk, for example, that our material resources are running out. We are implored to look to the needs of future generations. We selfishly "over-use" the gifts of creation. Our sins are now committed not against each other but against the earth. We need to rewrite the Ten Commandments that are only concerned about man and God.

The old Marxists, good Epicureans that they were, used to complain that concern with supernatural life was an impediment to our concentrating on this life. The energy devoted to useless things like worship and doctrine was better spent working at something useful. With everyone diligently laboring, we could produce a really good earth.

In one of his most devastating passages, Dostoyevsky said that, in the end, men will only ask for bread. That is, baking bread and such practical things are man's only purpose within the world. Once that choice is made, our worldly task will be to keep ourselves, or at least some yet-to-be-born folks not us, going for as long as possible in the future.

Things like globalization, ecology, international government, and population control thus become objects of intense political concern. Mankind's task becomes one of figuring out, on the basis of what we now know, what we can plan for in the distant future. Some say that we have the option of keeping a few people alive for a large number of millennia or causing the deaths of millions by using things on a short-term basis. Logically, there is not much difference in either of these views. It's just a question of how many and when.

Looking back at "creation," we can wonder how short-sighted the Lord was in creating us. Was it conceivable that the purpose of creation was to keep alive on this planet a certain number of our kind for as long as it kept twirling in space? Or was this "death" thing asking us to look in another direction?

Revelation suggests that mankind, like each member of the species, has an inner-worldly end. The earth is endowed with enough resources that man, by his own development of them, could meet the needs he has for a good life. To plan to go on and on is a kind of *hubris* that shifts attention away from what man is asked principally to do with his life; namely, save his soul.

This "saving one's soul" is a red flag for many who are committed to a save-the-earth-first philosophy, a view that subordinates man to cosmic and human forces, not vice versa.

Briefly, Christ came to save us from our sins, not to keep us floundering around forever in this world. How we will is what makes us closer or more distant from God in whatever age, since the beginning, in which we live.

CHAPTER 8

ON REALISM

POLITICAL realism originally meant that we did not expect too much from politics, or indeed from man, himself the agent of political action. Yet politics also meant that we did not expect too little either. All existing regimes show signs of both expectations. The Enlightenment heritage usually expected too much. Indeed, it promised eventually to provide a perfect world by eliminating recurrent wrongs. It would achieve this lofty goal by transforming economics, constitutions, psyches, or the environment. What was wrong was judged to be outside of man, not within him. The Machiavellian tradition, however, expected too little. It insisted that, to get things done, we had to do some evil, or at least we had to assign some prince or party to do the nasty tasks for us. All regimes were necessarily founded on the basis of allowing, even welcoming, some evil.

Most people remain perplexed that things seem to become worse even as we have all the access to information and technology that no previous generation could imagine. Often God gets the blame for this mess. Presumably he could have "fixed" things better in the beginning. In desperation, we hear of learned scientists wanting to redesign our bodies or to eliminate death entirely. Others claim that we need to flee to some outer space planet. We are consuming everything with which the earth has provisioned us. Otherwise, it's so long Charlie for the human race, what with global warming and other such lofty enthusiasms.

The realist tradition, which claims, among others, Thucydides, Aristotle, and Augustine, thought that such a thing as human nature existed. It held firm over time and space. Both dire and dignified deeds would recur pretty much in the same way every time human beings appeared, no matter how they configured themselves politically. We could find good folks in terrible regimes and bad apples in relatively good ones. Realists thought that, comparatively, we would always have rich and poor. Plato thought this to be the case also except, perhaps, in his city in speech. But it had no earthly location except in the mind of whoever wanted to think it through. We would always have a configuration of good and bad, usually, with eerie consistency. Citizens could be classified fairly accurately by Aristotle's virtues and vices or by the Ten Commandments taken in their bare essences.

Realists admitted that men existed to act among their peers. They needed to make things that people required and desired. The universe seemed already provisioned to provide for human needs and wants. But the astonishing thing was that to make useful and elegant things, man had to use his brains. Foraging in the fields and forests was not enough. He is the one creature who was required to think in order to not only provide for himself but also be what he ought to be. Certain standards or strands of nobility with which he was compared kept bothering his soul. In spite of his best efforts to eradicate any sense of an innate human nature, it keeps coming back. It was pretty clear to the sages of our kind that not only could things go wrong but they were likely to do so unless we worked to prevent it. Aristotle had not talked of habits for nothing.

This prevention of personal disorder, however, was premised on the fact that no automatic formula could be devised to guarantee that men must do what is right. The reason for this caveat seemed to imply that the rational animal had to choose to use his head. Right choice needed discipline and insight. But it was also clear that the actions of the worst of our kind also revealed a high level of cunning intelligence. Real tyrants were not dummies or just brutes. They were, as Plato taught us, philosopher-kings gone wrong. We miss the drama of our time if we fail to note the logic of decline that follows a relentless and systematic deviation from the good, almost as if to say that a more than human intelligence works against our true dignity.

But why did things go wrong? If it were necessary that they went wrong, we have no reason to blame anyone for anything. And as Aristotle also said, ethics and politics are matters of praise and blame, almost as if this judgment is an essential element in our lives together. Tell me what you praise or blame and I will tell you what you are. And if you do not tell me, I can usually figure it out by your actions, as you can mine. So it is realism we seek, the common sense that keeps away from both utopia and hell on earth, the realization that we have here no lasting city.

CHAPTER 9

ON CONTRADICTION

IN classical philosophy, human beings are called "rational animals." Why so? They are certainly animals with a
full range of sentient powers that are, in addition, directly
ordered to thinking. Man's knowing powers include everything about him doing what it is supposed to do. Curiously,
we find ourselves existing with a body, sensory powers,
and a mind. We did not give ourselves these things. We
woke up one morning to find them already there. A major
purpose in our lives is to figure out why we exist, or, better,
why we exist to know.

Evidently, once men appeared, they all had pretty much
the same powers. The advantage, if it is an advantage, of
coming later rather than earlier in time is that we also have
memories. We can recall and build on what others figured
out before us. The old cartoons that showed a bewildered
cave man pushing a wheelbarrow with a square wheel
instead of a round one made the point. Someone had to
invent the wheel. But once it was invented, not much use
or thrill was found in inventing it again, although we could
if we had to.

It is one thing to be given a mind and, to go along with
it, hands, those remarkable instruments that enable us to
connect our thoughts with something out there on which
to put them. We find that we can modify the things that are

out there. Tools enable us to do many things that would not be possible without our capacity to change things around to help us to achieve the end we want to effect. We are not totally wrong in thinking that perhaps it was intended this way.

Every so often we ask ourselves: "What is the mind for?" We seem to have it whether we like it or not. So we might as well take a look at it. We call this look self-reflection, which is the only way we can get at it. No doubt mind has baffled more than one philosopher throughout the ages.

Initially, the most peculiar thing about our minds is their seeming constant prodding to know what something is or isn't. Kids drive their parents crazy with such questions about what is this or that? When a Chinese mother tells her child the thing is a chair, the Chinese word is not the same as the word of the Latvian mother who says the same thing in Latvian. But the answer, whether in Mandarin or Latvian, indicates the same thing, something to sit on. Next we learn that sitting is not standing or lying down. We distinguish words and what they mean.

Our minds enable us to know things other than ourselves and our immediate wants. Indeed, they enable us to know just about anything that comes along if we set our minds to it. We want to know, *pace* Socrates, what is not ourselves. We soon find out one thing that we cannot do. We cannot say that Joe is John. We have to say Joe is not John. We can say Joe is an Englishman. John is an Englishman. We cannot say an Englishman is a Latvian. So abstractions also at some level differ as do particular things. We affirm the distinctions.

The mind has one overarching "principle" that enables someone with a mind to think properly. This is the principle of contradiction. It is usually stated that a thing cannot be and not be at the same time in the same circumstances. If two things were identical in everything, including their existence, they would be the same being and the question of difference could never arise.

How do I know that this principle is true? Not because someone told me it was. It is because I cannot think it not true without at the same time affirming that it is true. With this principle, I can begin to distinguish and separate things. I can begin to put some order into things. This thing is not that thing. This thing is like that thing, but it is different too.

We do not want to deceive ourselves about what is out there. Plato said that the worst thing that could happen to us is willingly to have a lie in our soul about *what is*. A lie is when we know one thing but affirm another thing about it. When we contradict ourselves, when we say of something that is, that it is not, we display to ourselves and to others with minds a malfunctioning in our own mind.

Contradictions will not leave us alone. At the highest level, we are not, and know we are not, being what we ought to be if we maintain them. This is the blessing of the principle of contradiction. It won't let us alone. This is probably why we have it.

CHAPTER 10

ON THE FATE OF JESUIT DONKEYS

WHEN I arrived back in Los Gatos from Georgetown, I mentioned in a column (*Catholic Thing*, April 18, 2013) that on this property we had five "jackasses." They were denizens of the land. I recounted that they were in a field above the house and had followed me down a trail one afternoon to their feeding pen. This scene occasioned some learned comments from the brethren about the nature of Schall's "following."

In the meantime, two of the jennies (female donkeys) had foals, cute little critters in fact. The jack, not a practicing monogamist, and the two jennies, unlike mules, proved to be quite adept at reproducing their kind. The donkeys became a center of local curiosity. We have trails through the property with "No Trespassing" signs on the fences.

These donkeys had no obvious purpose. I once suggested to the superior that we open a business of giving two-dollar donkey rides as a means of support. He thought it a splendid idea and shrewdly appointed Schall to run the operation. No more was ever heard of this otherwise brilliant proposal.

Thanks to its Italian Jesuit founding in the nineteenth century, this institution had a winery ("Novitiate of Los Gatos") with acres of grape fields. Donkeys were used to plough the steep hillsides behind the house. Today, the donkeys are more in the order of pets. And that is the origin of their sad fate that I will now recount. It is a classic example of what happens in an overly-legalized society.

One afternoon, I was walking down one of the hills. A rather upset lady stopped me. She complained that the donkeys were emaciated. We Jesuits were starving them. Naturally, I claimed innocence of any deliberate tendency to "donkey-cide." Edgar, the local keeper of the animals, assured me that the donkeys were well-fed and watered. They grazed contentedly on the grassy slopes around the house.

Many people would come up. They gave the donkeys human food that, while well intentioned, was not really good for them. Rumor had it that this lady took the issue to the Humane Society. Superiors imagined headlines in the local paper: "Jesuits Starve Donkeys."

But this was only the beginning. Particularly after the baby donkeys were born, mothers would bring little kids up to see them. The more agile ones would climb over the fence to pet and hug the donkeys. It was a charming scene. The kids loved it.

Donkeys, however, are animals. This is a first principle, as Aristotle said. They can kick, bite, and slobber. Again the specter of enterprising lawyers came up. Even with "No Trespassing" signs, if some little kid were kicked by a donkey, the headlines would read: "Jesuit Donkey Kicks Local Youth." You see the problem?

To anticipate the worst-case scenario is a function of the human mind. So, following Ignatius of Loyola's rules for decision-making, it was determined to find another home for our good donkeys. Even with every precaution taken, there is little possibility today of escaping oodles of law-suits in such a possible situation.

So the prudence of this world determined that the don-key-keepers look around for other farms that would pur-chase or take the animals. Places were soon enough found. Donkey friendships and families were broken up. The threats of lawyers rule the land.

Now our property no longer hears the familiar "Hee-Haw" of the jack to wake up a slumbering Jesuit or provide a good conversation at lunch. Our place is now more silent. We once had some horses and chickens on this land, but, like the donkeys, are no more.

From my youth, I recalled my uncles' farms when they still had smaller family farms in Iowa. I remember vividly the farm sounds—cows, horses, mules, hens, roosters, cats, dogs, bulls, hogs, sheep, turkeys, tractors, windmills, not to mention the birds and field animals. I remember yarns about hearing corn grow on hot summer nights. Today we hear the noise of the highway to Santa Cruz below, air-planes above, cell phones everywhere. What was the name of that song? "Sounds of silence"?

Donkeys appear in Scripture. King David rode a don-key. Jesus himself rode one into Jerusalem on Palm Sun-day. Mary is said to have ridden a donkey into Egypt. I read somewhere of a Muslim rule that Christians could not ride horses but had to use donkeys.

Donkeys are famous "beasts of burden" in mountains and tough trails. They are sure-footed. Presumably they share with mules the quality of stubbornness, for which quality something is to be said.

Is Cecil the African lion's story sadder than the legal shadow over our donkey family? I would not venture to estimate. Animal "rights" and "liabilities" these days have strange consequences even in the now more silent hills above Los Gatos.

CHAPTER 11

ON THE FUTURE

THE future often has a bad reputation. "In the long run, we'll all be dead." No actual beings exist in the future. The past is all over. The future has not come around. It need not. The only real thing is the present, which keeps changing. The advantage the past has over the future is that, at one time, actual, not imaginary, human beings walked about, folks with names. They did things. We grasp what human beings are like by looking at what they did or did not do, or what they did do but shouldn't have.

The theory of progress once assured us that things necessarily become better. By redefining evil out of existence, by historicizing it, some can still think progress is automatic. Paradise thus is down the ages, in this world's future. We can hardly wait to arrive there. We put all our energies in the future. We want to shed the present messiness. We educate the young about the future, not the past. They thus remain largely clueless. The only trouble is that most of us, like our ancient and recent ancestors, won't make it to this anticipated, blissfully happy future.

This progressive view is the opposite of that often depicted in the classics. They thought the world was pretty good in the beginning, like the Garden of Eden but without the Tree in it to rile things up. Yet, while many things seem better as future becomes past, a gnawing sense spreads.

Things are getting progressively worse. We hear apocalypse more often than we hear utopia. The world betrays
multiple "deviations" from the good, not an untroubled
"progress" to something perfect.

The circular view of history—as, say, in Thucydides—
tells us that things will come around again and again in
pretty much the same way as they did on their first tour. In
the cyclic order of change, all things become intelligible
to us. In the extreme form, over time we become everyone else. We even become ourselves a second or third time
around. It is difficult to see how someone who holds such
a theory does not end in despair—"You mean this is all
there is?"

Many authors from J. B. Bury (d. 1927) on have pointed
out that our envisioned inner-worldly future is, on reflection, but a secularized version of Christian eschatology.
Heaven, hell, death, and purgatory are not such odd ideas
after all when we see how they become transformed into
political, economic, and ecological goals. Heaven becomes
what we create down the ages. Hell is any opposition to it.
Death is overcome by cloning or science. Purgatory is what
we must endure just before perfection.

Religion, especially Christianity, is hated because it
insists that each man's end transcends the world. The purpose of secularized man in the world is finally to produce
a perfect society (a "heaven") through human intelligence
and enterprise alone. Its model is humanity minus God. But
this coming perfection is in some "future," however near or
distant. The billions of people who lived before the arrival
of this goal, which includes all of us, will have lived as
tools for future generations whenever they come along.

In the Christian view, from the beginning a divine plan and order exists in the events of the world. No one was created solely as a means for someone else's happiness. Whether one is born at the beginning, middle, or end of history, each individual life is, before God, in the same position as every other life. Each person chooses his transcendent status through the life given to him.

It is said of Judas, something not said of anyone else, that it would "have been better if he were not born" (Mt 26:24). Today's world, of course, is filled with infants who would be better left to be born. Those who connive to prevent them, unless forgiven, are probably the ones who come closest to the judgment about Judas.

Our world is a battle scene of three eschatologies: ecological/humanist, Muslim, and Christian. The battle analogy is apt. The humanists save the earth for some generation down the ages. The Muslims submit all to the will of Allah whether they like it or not. The Christians do not doubt the "vale of tears" we live in. The end of each person is transcendent. It includes death. It is the inner Trinitarian life of God in which each person is invited to participate. But it can be rejected in the way we think and live.

Josef Pieper reflects on a fourth "eschatology"; namely, the "catastrophic end of history within time," the one that Scripture seems to suggest. He describes it as a "universal totalitarian regime of evil." "It will be we ourselves who bring about the end of history." We are not to despair, but this may well be our inner-worldly future.

CHAPTER 12

THE FIRST DAY OF SPRING

EXACTLY four years ago on the first day of spring, I left Washington to come here to Los Gatos in California. The day of departure, the spring equinox, was deliberately chosen. The days become longer; though, in the Southern Hemisphere, they become shorter. We spend our passing lives on a planet that continually turns on its axis, dips forward and backward with the seasons. All the while it follows a millions of mile elliptical orbit around the Sun, our Sun, not somebody else's. We don't own it. In a way, it owns us. None of us had the slightest thing to do with its being there, in making it possible for our kind to exist and to draw out our days—though in never quite the same springs, summers, falls, and winters.

During the first years out here, we had severe droughts, made worse both by "earth-warming" and by California's fifty-year neglect of its infrastructure as well as by its ideological policies. This year, we have had bountiful rains, made possible, again, by "earth warming." (N.B., This is California; we can have it both ways.) In preparation for the next drought, never far away, the storms' run-off waters were again not adequately collected behind dams never built.

Across from us, the Mt. Diablo and Mt. Hamilton Ranges rise above the tip of San Francisco Bay and the Santa Clara

Valley (once known as Prune Valley, now as Silicon Valley). The visible hillsides and woods continue into and over the nearby Santa Cruz Mountains. They separate us from Monterey Bay and the Pacific some fifteen miles away. The hills all glisten with a delicate light green, almost unbearably beautiful at times as different configurations of clouds, winds, sunrises, sunsets, and time of day bring to life some corner of this world that we had never noticed before.

Noticing is one of the most important things about us. Or to put it negatively, our lives are filled with myriads of things we never paid attention to. We couldn't mark all of them. Oftentimes, however, someone else did notice, which is why, I suspect, we have literature and memory. But it is a good thing to come to terms with our finitude. We suspect, ultimately, that it does not have the last word.

In his *Grammar*, N. M. Gwynne wrote, "Traditionally, the purpose of the fine arts, in which poetry, literature, is, of course, one, has not been considered to be one of self-indulgence, but of trying to make the world a better place, in however small a degree" (125). That is a telling sentence. It is mindful of a theme in Tolkien that the great deeds of this world are not always accomplished by the great ones but often by some unknown wayfarer in some unsuspected corner of the world.

The notion of "making the world a better place" sounds almost trite today when we have little agreement about what we mean by "better," though Gwynne's term "self-indulgent" still gives a pretty good idea of what we do not want to be. "Self-indulgence" does not mean that we cannot enjoy a good beer or dessert. It means that we can enjoy them because we know where they fit into the kind of lives we have been given.

If we look about us, most of the once well-known vices are now considered at least "rights," if not crimes to oppose, let alone to define them accurately. Indeed, it is called "making the world a better place," if we do not look too carefully at what actually goes on. We define our babies out of existence so that we can have compassion and, simultaneously, remove any grounds from the next wave of compassion that will soon eliminate anyone who is defined as less than perfect.

Love, they say, means looking to the good of another. That "looking" usually means "sacrificing for." It means the effort to be virtuous. It also means the constant effort to know the truth of things. It means not to lie about them. They say that virtue is its own reward, but so is vice. The self-indulgent man wants everyone else to love him for his own sake. He is convinced that he deserves it. How quaint!

What else do we know about spring? A friend's sister tried hiking in the Georgia mountains with her twenty-one-year-old athletic grandniece. But they turned back. "I'm indescribably tired. And cold. And freezing," she explained to her sister. "'Know thyself,' a wise man said. So I know now that I will never be doing the three-month Appalachian Trail ever in my life. Ain't gonna happen." Another thing to notice about our lives—they betray certain limitations. This awareness is *not* self-indulgence. It is prudence. It is metaphysics. It is making the world a better place.

CHAPTER 13

ON RECONSIDERING THE SOUTHERN CAUSE

"If we examine Lee first upon the art at which he surpassed, we find a curiously dispassionate understanding not just of technique, but of the place of war in the life of civilized man. Napoleon too was a philosopher of battle, but his utterances are mixed with cynicism. Those of Lee have always the saving grace of affirmation. Let us mount with the General the height above Fredericksburg and hear from him one of the most searching observations ever made. It is contained in a brief remark, so innocent-seeming, expressed as he gazed upon the field of slain on that December day. 'It is well this is terrible; otherwise we should grow fond of it.'"

—Richard Weaver, "Lee as a Philosopher"[2]

MANY people watched the so-called Southern battle flag lowered from the South Carolina statehouse. This flag was relatively new, not really a designated flag of the Southern armies. The South had at least three other official flags. The so-called Confederate battle flag, used by

---

[2] Essay first appeared in *The Georgia Review*, Fall 1948, reprinted in *The Southern Essays of Richard Weaver*.

two units in the Army of Northern Virginia, was not flown over the South Carolina statehouse until 1961 when other battles were taking place. On most of the programs that I heard in the current controversy, almost everyone claimed, as if totally obvious, that slavery was the only cause of the Civil War.

But people like Lord Acton, Chesterton, and many others, early on, saw the American Civil War in other lights. While they did not condone slavery, neither did they think that slavery was the sole, or even the most important, cause. Recent top-down impositions by the central state make their concerns, in retrospect, look almost prophetic. The principal concern, in the view of many, was the ability to protect a family or city from a statist ideology or culture that would impose its will on every segment of the country.

Secession, as a constitutional theory, was thought to be the final legal and political defense against the imposition of arbitrary power. The victory of the North, in this sense, settled the issue by blood, not by argument. From this angle, Lincoln was not looked on as a hero but as the harbinger of the absolute state in which presidential directives, not Congress or the people, ruled. Today we add the court to this issue of imposing unconstitutional power on the people and the states.

To insist that the only cause of the war was slavery—and it was a cause of the war—obscures a number of things. People still argue whether war was the best or only way to eliminate slavery. Others think that economics, not politics or war, was the real cause of slavery's end. If we look at many of the reactions to the Supreme Court's imposition of its will on the nation in cases since at least *Griswold* and *Roe* to *Casey* and *Obergefell,* we see a rather desperate search for grounds to resist this imposition of arbitrary power by the central government on its states and citizens. Some state legislatures and governors, such as Oklahoma, are seeking a way to resist this imposition. Other approaches include a conscious withdrawal from participation in the state that now controls almost the whole public order and most of its institutions. The churches themselves are now facing the distinct possibility that the price of their public presence is conformity to the state's laws and what they demand.

This resistance is not just "civil rights." It arises from natural law. We need to read carefully again Hadley Arkes's book *Beyond the Constitution* to appreciate what the real issues are. The higher law tradition of our civilization has always assumed that state laws themselves are only legitimate when they do not violate natural law. When they do, they are invalid. The question then becomes how does one "resist" them when secession is excluded? The state has the power and uses it as if no higher law than itself exists. This usage divides the citizenry into two segments: 1) state law, whatever it does, as the highest law and 2) the state as limited to what is reasonable.

But another aspect of this issue is worth considering. We now see movements to remove statues and names given to monuments and schools of southern figures—Jefferson Davis, Robert E. Lee, Stonewall Jackson, and others. What we are witnessing in these actions is the rejection of the honorable and dignified peace that Lincoln, Grant, and others insisted on making to end the war.

Most people acknowledge that the reconstruction was full of corruption and greed on the part of the victors, that its spirit created a basis for rejecting the spirit of the peace. Ending any war and establishing a workable peace are often more important than winning the war. Many wars have been lost at the peace tables.

What I see appears to be a vengeful elimination of any memory or dignity in the South, a dignity the peace after the Civil War thought it wise to allow. This same vengeful spirit imposes state law on a society. It was crucial to the peace after the Civil War to leave the South with a sense of dignity, with their lost cause. The South was not seen to be so totally vilified that only moral monsters could remain. They had to be eliminated as devils. Lee was not a moral monster. As his colleagues in the Northern forces recognized, he had his nobility. His example of retiring to private life, to Washington College, was one of the main reasons that the war ended in the honorable fashion it did. It ended in surrender and return to peaceful ways, not in extended backwoods fighting and harassment.

Removing any signs of the existence of a Southern Cause, seeing only its hated "peculiar institution" has its irony. It comes at a time when the other side of the Southern Cause, its concern about unlimited central power able and willing to impose its ideology on everyone, is, for many, at the center of our attention. Without secession and without an army, many look for ways to withdraw from this state power. They want to practice what they hold to be true. An unforgiving relentlessness appears in this imposition of power. It is mindful of the efforts to remove any sign of dignity in the Southern Cause to see only evil in it.

The spirit of the day at Appomattox was dignified finality and forgiveness. This ending allowed hard fighting men to return to their homes if they could. They did not demand vengeance and war crimes. Most people since the war's end have seen the wisdom of this decision.

So, rightly or wrongly, I see the events around the South Carolina statehouse in a different way. It seems to be blind to any nobility that Lincoln wisely hoped to leave in the South in its defeat. We witness the arrival of that counter-spirit of absolute state power that a few saw rising in the North as its unfolding spirit.

As many of their most basic assumptions are now rejected at the most fundamental level, we see the shadows of what once concerned the Old South. The term *slavery* takes on a new image. The masters are civil officials. A more dangerous and demanding enemy shows itself. It does not just demand that we stay in the Union. We must also agree with its laws as "rights" that must be obeyed as the price of citizenship.

CHAPTER 14

COMMON GOOD AND
UNCOMMON EVIL

O F late, I have heard much about the "common good" but little about "common evil." The common good does not mean that some substantial form exists out there which we are trying to embody perfectly in our dealings with one another. Such an idea is responsible for much serious evil in the modern world. Rather, the common good signifies that order in which human persons and groups of persons, bound by some common purpose, can themselves flourish because of their own reason, habits, and freedom. It does not mean that everyone does the same things or has the same tasks, talents, rewards, or burdens. It means that they do not. Thus, a wide variety of riches in every area can freely come forth.

Plato's specialization requires our recognizing that we cannot do everything by ourselves. If we do so try, we all will be poorer. Man, as a political animal, should establish an order in which the particular goods of each person are achieved through work, through fair exchange for the goods of others. The state is not itself a common good or a substantial being but an order in which, through action, goods can be brought forth and distributed by sensible human beings. The process is not magic.

But "common evil"? Evil, in the classic sense, is the absence of a good that ought to be there but is not. Hence, evil is not a thing but the *lack* of something that ought to be there in a good thing. Moral evil means the deliberate failure to put a right measure in our freely chosen actions or words. Evil cannot exist except in some good. Hence, when we bring "good" out of "evil," we do not make what is evil good. Rather, we take what is already good in the being that does evil and develop it. This is what repentance is about. It admits that the original good was indeed good. Evil, as such, can never become good, nor good evil.

Yet, as Christians, we sense that something more needs to be said. Evil is more than a philosophic concern about "lacks," though it is that too. Evil seems personal. Someone wants to discuss it with us, wants to convince us evil is good. Pope Francis has said that the devil "hates" us. Blunt words. Francis is not talking about some inert "lack." He is talking about a positive hating of the good because it is good.

Classical ethics and moral philosophy gave us accounts of virtues and vices. Usually two vices existed for every virtue, one that erred on the side of too much and the other, too little. We do find in the writings of Plato a sense that our vices are not just foibles or mistakes but objects of judgment. Plato rightly worried that the world was created in injustice if the vices were not ultimately punished. This consideration led him to propose the immortality of the soul to guarantee that no one could get away with doing evil even if he died in human glory but covered with sins.

Christianity provided a more profound explanation of evil though one not necessarily disagreeing with Plato.

Christ affirmed that the devil's kingdom could not stand if it had dissention within its ranks. This information meant, as I understand it, both that we find a logical sequence of disorders, or deviations from the good, as Aristotle understood, and an active presence. This logic works through willing human beings who find themselves assenting to a step-by-step deviation from the good, each worse than the one before.

Those familiar with spiritual literature recall that the Church Fathers warned monks that sin begins with things only slightly off-center. Yet things do not stand still. Either the evil is recognized and corrected or the next logical step away from the good is taken. Eventually this leads to calling of evil good, all in the name of pursuing some good but in a manner contrary to reason or the commandments.

What I take to be "common evil" today exists in our public order as a "hatred" of the good that is embodied in innocent human life and the way in which it ought to exist. It seems clear that the ultimate "hatred" is for innocent human life in its weakest conditions. When we look at the steps that justify this position, we cannot help but seeing a steady pattern of deviation that leads politicians, judges, experts, professors, and ordinary people along a deviant line. Finally, they justify lying to themselves that they work for the "common good" when, in fact, they freely promote "uncommon evil."

CHAPTER 15

ON THE ABORTED

HOW does one think of the aborted? They are not abstractions, however tiny. They constitute a significant proportion of all human beings called into existence. We have no monuments or graves to commemorate their being here. Their bodies are said to have "commercial" use or can be used to "aid" others to improve their lives. So they are not "nothing." Their elimination must be "justified."

Each human being begins at conception and lasts until that initial life force ends in death, say, four score and ten years later if not sooner, much sooner for the aborted. Many human lives never reach birth for reasons of sickness, accidents, or malformation. We call them miscarriages. The immediate cause of their death was not a willed human intervention.

Karl Rahner wrote, "'To be born' means to come into existence without being asked." An abortion terminates a begun human life by human agency. The aborted or its agency is again not asked or considered. Murder is the unjust destruction of an already born human being at the hands of another, again without the victim's being asked. The aborted have the act ending their lives "done unto them."

We are not "asked" whether we want to be born or not. That is a great thing, really. Existence and even the desire to exist are, in fact, not in our hands. They are gifts. What is in our hands is the life of what is begotten of human parents, male and female.

So what is the "status" of those unborn members of the human race who are, in fact, killed by other human beings, those whose ostensible responsibility is to protect them and bring them to birth and maturity?

Estimates vary but we are told that, worldwide, some forty-two million individuals are aborted each year. This figure is probably a minimum and has been repeating itself each year for decades. It is well-known that girls are more likely to be aborted than boys, so abortion skewers normal ratios of men to women.

Many, if not most, citizens have no doubt grown "comfortable" with such numbers. Not a few are more likely to be concerned over the death of pets than over that of the aborted human child. Why is this? In one sense, it is true that every aborted child is "unwilled." It is unwanted at least to the degree that its incipient life fails to prevent some parent, doctor, or official from killing it should those who are naturally responsible for it will that they do not wish to deal with the already-present child.

For a long while, in this matter, everything was done to lie to ourselves about what was being aborted. We had long, supposedly scientific, explanations about how human life was not there yet. But these days are over. No one can really claim that what is aborted is not a human being in its first stages, a stage we all passed through. We have videos that simply show this unified sequence from conception.

Every human being who ever lived was once in the same condition. The argument, if it is an argument, now accepts that what is killed is human. "Rights talk" makes it possible for us, however, to speak of lives that "should" not exist. The human race now claims authority to decide who lives and who dies. Some actual human beings are not "human" enough to live. To get rid of them has something "noble" about it, like saving the race from itself.

Yet I want to look at the aborted from another angle. We sometimes say of martyrs that they died for a noble cause. We do not recognize that "the aborted" represent a significant part of the human race, that part which is killed by our choice not to have them among us. But who are they? Both the aborted and those who manage to be born have the same ultimate origin. Each human life begins in conception. The human soul does not cause itself to exist. The origin of each human life is ultimately in the Godhead. Each is an image of God intended for eternal life. This eternal life includes each aborted child no matter at what stage its demise was decreed by another who does not allow him to continue to exist in this world.

But in that sense, it is too late. It already exists in this world. The total number of human beings to exist—perhaps some hundred billion thus far on this planet—includes the aborted. It also includes those who aborted them directly or indirectly—the doctors, the politicians. Those who kill the aborted are generally not called to judgment in the courts of this world. But the world is created in ultimate justice. The aborted exist for eternal life, but also to identify who killed them. The aborted remain members of the human race with all the dead. Without being asked, they are killed. Their lives are not "nothing."

CHAPTER 16

THE GREAT THIRST

IN *The Range of Reason*, Jacques Maritain wrote, "The world is prey to a great thirst, an immense mystical yearning which does not even know itself and which, because it remains without objective, turns to despair or neurosis." Most people easily comprehend the notion of a great "thirst." Thirst concentrates our attention. If thirst is great, we do not ask, "What quenches our thirst?" We know. The "object" of our physical need is "water, cool clear water," as the Sons of the Pioneers used to sing.

Other beverages, like lemonade, can also subdue our dry throats. Chesterton said that people, after a long, hot, walk on a dusty English road, do not drink beer because of its alcohol. Beer is a drink. We are thirsty. In normal thirst, what we most want is simply water. Since beer is mostly water, it can satisfy our thirst. A martini or a brandy, in the same circumstances, would not do the trick. Indeed, either would probably increase our thirst for water. "Why is there both water and thirst in the universe?" we might wonder.

What is interesting about Maritain's remarks is the analogy to another kind of "thirst," one for something other than water. This is not an argument from desire to existence, but from existence to desire. This "mystical yearning" does not know itself. Unlike normal thirst, this deeper thirst does not know its object straightaway. What is it that will satisfy us?

If I am dying of thirst, no one has any doubt about what it is that I want and need. We are judged in the Gospels by whether we give a cup of water to someone in need. But the need and what satisfies it are so obvious that no further explanation is necessary. If someone is really thirsty, we do not inquire of him, "Why do you keep talking about water?" We know what he needs. We still may not give it to him. The latter problem is not that we do not know what he needs.

Maritain's comment has two points: 1) we have a longing for something that we are not quite able fully to identify, and 2) this "object" we seek is rather like water is to thirst. That is, it is something very real, something that responds to the "thirst" that we experience in our souls. These reflections are very Augustinian.

But notice how Maritain used the verb *prey*. Since we do not know the exact object of this search, "face-to-face" as it were, we go off in all sorts of strange directions searching for it in places where it cannot be found. Augustine said that we confuse beautiful things for Beauty itself.

But when we do not find what we are thirsting for, "despair and neurosis" can result. Many thinkers suspect that the disordered souls that we see everywhere around us are caused by this "despair and neurosis" that result from not knowing or not wanting to know the real object that can transform our search the way water transforms a thirsty man. Are we then left with no light here, no knowledge of the object of this ultimate thirst that we all experience in ourselves whether we admit it or not?

The problem arises, I think, from what we are created to be. We simply are not created for any other purpose but

that of being invited to live, yes, forever, the inner life of
the Triune God. No one, nowhere, is created for any other
purpose. Everything we encounter in existence, including
ourselves, has an immediate purpose to be *what it is*. We
are human beings, not turtles. That mountain is a mountain, not a redwood tree, even if redwood trees grow on
mountains.

The "thirst" that we all carry about in our very being will
not leave us alone. We will search, test, and try everything
we run into. We find out that each finite thing is good all
right. But it does not fully settle us down. "Why?" we ask.
If we are made to find that "object" that does satisfy us,
why were we not informed about it in more detail?

The fact is that we were and are informed about it, and in
pretty vivid detail. The drama of our "despair and neurosis"
is not that we were neglected by the source of our being.
We weren't. The problem is that we have to come to the
final "object" of our thirst in the way that was handed down
to us. We make up many alternatives, mostly odd projections of our own minds. But somehow they do not "work."
Without the "thirst," we could not be *what we are*. With it,
we can only be satisfied by the divine life after the manner
it was given to us to receive.

CHAPTER 17

WHAT IS MUSIC?

A FTER he left the papacy, Benedict XVI declined receiving any honorary academic degrees. But recently he made an exception. He accepted an invitation from the Academy of Music in Krakow in Poland. This was the school of his old friend and predecessor, Pope John Paul II, who, as we recall, loved to sing. In the course of these ceremonies at Pope Benedict's residence in the Vatican, he gave a brief but profound talk on "music and truth," in which he asked the question "What is music?" As if to remind us of Benedict's own capacity to answer this very question, *L'Ossrevatore Romano* shows a photo of Benedict, in white cassock, seated at his piano obviously playing some piece of classical music. We also might recall, as the philosopher Leo Strauss used to insist, that "What is?" questions stand at the heart of the mind's relation to reality. We long to know what things are. We need to think them through.[3]

The issue that Benedict addressed was whether the music in the West was different and, if so, why. I want to approach the comments of Benedict through some reflections that the French philosopher Pierre Manent recently made in his *Seeing Things Politically* about "What is the

---

[3]   Benedict XVI, "Music and Truth," *L'Osservatore Romano*, English, August 14, 2015.

West?"[4] Basically, the issue comes down to the question of whether anything unique is found about the Western intellectual heritage that is not just "western" but also universal. That is to say, "Are all cultures the same so that all cultures are relatively equal?" When sorted out, this is the classic issue of relativism and historicism; namely, the assumption that no objective truth can be found in things. No "universal" culture exists. All is relative to time and place. Hence, we cannot address the question of the "truth" or lack of it that is found in any culture, religion, or country.

"The Greeks clearly conceived of a radically different way to say what a human being is other than telling stories," Manent wrote. "The Greeks taught us that, rather than telling stories, it is possible to consider the *being* of things, the *being* of humans; it is possible to *theorein*, to look at *what is* with the eye of the mind." This understanding of the capacity to know recalls what Benedict said in his "Regensburg Lecture" about the importance of Paul being called precisely to Macedonia, to the Greeks, the home of the philosophers. As a basis for dealing with all subsequent cultures and religions on a common basis, it was important first to establish the relation of Christian revelation to mind as understood by the Greeks. Such thought was understood not as "Greek mind" but as mind as such. The truths contained in both philosophy and revelation could be coherently related.[5]

---

4   Pierre Manent, *Seeing Things Politically* (South Bend: St. Augustine's Press, 2015), 171-74.

5   See James V. Schall, *The Regensburg Lecture* (South Bend: St. Augustine's Press, 2007); *Political Philosophy & Revelation: A Catholic View* (Washington: The Catholic University of America Press, 2012).

"What," we might ask, "does this reflection have to do with music?" Benedict begins his response by recalling his youth when he would attend the great German Masses in the churches of Salzburg, those of Mozart, Bach, Handel, Bruckner, and Beethoven. (Robert Reilly, in his *Surprised by Beauty,* discusses in more detail the question of sacred music and reminds us that much sacred music has been written in recent decades). Benedict cites especially Mozart's *Missa della incarnazione.* Benedict points out that the Second Vatican Council never intended to minimize such glorious church music. He betrays a touch of annoyance at those liturgists who insisted that these great concert Masses were fit only for the concert hall and not for Mass as they were intended; that is, at actual celebrated Masses with a congregation.

It is at this point that Benedict asks himself: "What, in fact, is music?" We are again reminded of the clarity of this pope's mind. "Where does (music) come from? And to what does it aspire?" We listen to music of various kinds, but we seldom ask about its nature, its source or purpose. Benedict suggests three places from which music "flows." The first is the "experience of love." People are "seized" by love. When this happens, they begin to see "another dimension" of reality. "Poetry, song, and music in general arise from being struck . . . from this opening to a new dimension of life."[6] Aristotle had said that when a lover of the flute hears its sound, he stops everything to listen to it. He is

---

6   See James V. Schall, *The Classical Moment: Essays in Knowledge and Its Pleasures* (South Bend: St. Augustine's Press, 2013).

struck by it. Love is not content with its own happening but wants to manifest itself, sing of it.

The second source of music is "sadness." On the page of *L'Osservatore Romano* on which the photo of Benedict at the piano is shown, there is also a printed sheet of music which contains the notes of a famous medieval hymn by Jacapone di Todi, the very poignant *Dies Irae*, music often sung in the old funeral rites. Such music we often find also in spirituals and western music when words are not sufficient to express one's sorrow or sadness. I think of Johnny Cash's "Sunday Morning Comin' Down" or the Seldom Scene's "The Ballad of the Rebel Soldier."

The third source of music is "the encounter with the divine which from the very beginning is part of what defines humanity." This kind of music indicates a new experience for man. It is the encounter with the "wholly other." This encounter inspires our kind to a new height and form of "expression." Indeed, Benedict suspects that in songs of love and sadness we already find intimations of music addressed to God. These experiences in song are not themselves complete without sensing the divine presence in our loves and sorrows. This sense of God is, then, the "overall origin of music." Benedict in particular points to the Psalms as examples of song and music at its best. "The quality of music depends on the purity and greatness of the encounter with the divine, with the experience of love and pain."

Benedict has clearly been thinking of these things. He has been thinking of music in relation to the way differing cultures are now aware of and encounter each other. This reflection is what brings us back to the Manent remarks on "What is the West?" In most cultures, we have literature, sculpture, painting, architecture, and music. "In no other cultural environment, however, does the greatness of music equal that born in the sphere of the Christian faith, from Palestrina to Bach, from Handel to Mozart, Beethoven and Bruckner. The music of the West is something unique, which has no equal in other cultures. That should make us think." What is it about this music that makes it different? I believe there are millions of Chinese students studying Western classical music.

Benedict acknowledges that more than sacred music exists in the West. But the "deepest" source of the uniqueness of Western music is found in the liturgy, "in the encounter with God." Benedict adds, "In the works of Bach, for whom this glory of God ultimately represented the aim of all music, this is quite evident." Benedict's conclusion parallels the end of Benedict's great work *Jesus of Nazareth*, a book that examined whether any other plausible understanding of Scripture could be possible except that Christ was who he said he was. "The great and pure response of Western music was developed in the encounter with a God who, in the liturgy, is rendered present to us in Jesus Christ."

Benedict adds a surprising conclusion: "I feel that music is a demonstration of the truth of Christianity. Wherever such a response develops, there has been an encounter with Truth, with the true Creator of the world. For this reason, great sacred music is a reality of theological rank and of permanent significance for the faith of the whole of Christianity, even if it is by no means necessary that it be performed always and everywhere." It remains a way to participate in the celebration of the "mystery of faith." The fact is that most Christians are deprived of the beauty of the music in the liturgical context that Benedict so poignantly and beautifully describes.

Where such music is present, there is the West. But it is not just the geographic West. It is the locus of reason and music whose root is the divine, in the *Missa della incarnazione*. Beauty and truth are what attract all men to sing to the glory of God, both in their loves and in their sadnesses. "What is the West?" "What is music?"—these intimately related questions are resolved in the reality of who Jesus Christ is, in the realization that the Incarnation happened amongst us. It is about this that we sing in the liturgy.

CHAPTER 18

THE TRINITY

"Truth is so obscure in these times, and falsehood so established, that unless we love the truth, we cannot know it."
—Pascal, *Pensées*, no. 863

"So when the Son of God became the Son of Man, the Spirit also descended upon him, becoming accustomed in this way to dwelling with the human race, to living in men and to inhabiting God's creation. The Spirit accomplished the Father's will in men who had grown old in sin, and gave them new life in Christ."
—Irenaeus, *Against Heresies*, 3, 17

I

OFTEN it is said that Christianity is too complicated. It is too intellectual. Would it not be more effective if it only had five simple things to maintain, like Islam? Why cannot we just be "nice" and forget about all these complicated distinctions? In response to such a query, Chesterton once pointed out that Christianity is simple where reality is simple, but it is not simple where reality is not simple, or at least, not simple to us. If "being nice" is your principle of morality, you had better be sure that everyone agrees on what the phrase means. That "agreement" would have to rest on principles that everyone understood. The "obscurity" of truth, to which Pascal referred, may be due to our own limited capacities. To God, the truth is not obscure. The problem is that we are not gods, which is quite all right. We were never intended to be "like gods" with power to decide good and evil. It was the devil who tried to convince Eve that we were like the gods.

Human beings usually have to learn things one step at a time, not in one blind flash. And some things, such as "What is the inner life of God like?" we can only know if we are assisted by God's help. If we could figure it out by ourselves, we would already be gods. But it is pretty sure that we are not gods. As the Psalmist says, we are "a little lower than the angels." That is why Irenaeus said that it takes the Spirit to accomplish the Father's will among us sinners. It is why Pascal said that some things we cannot properly "know" unless we love them.

If we take a careful look at the elements of the statement of Irenaeus, the great second century bishop from Lyons in Gaul, we find the following words and phrases: "Son of God," "Son of Man," "Spirit," "Father," "sin," "new life," and "Christ." To understand these words, and that is why we have minds, we have to think, think carefully and clearly about them. Christian revelation was given to us also that we think about what is told to us in various ways through the deeds and words in Scripture. The assumption is that how we live is related to what we know. The most obvious question we have on reading such a passage from

Irenaeus is "How does it fit together?" "How are these concepts related to each other?"

To begin to understand what Irenaeus is telling us, something he himself has clearly already meditated on, we need to know that "the Son of God" is "the Son of Man." The same person, called by two different names, is both one and the other. How this dual designation is possible is what the Incarnation was about. In becoming man, the Son of God did not cease to be God. He also "became" man. The Church later expressed this position by saying that two "natures," one divine and one human, are found in one Person who is divine, called the Son of God.

Why is the word *son* used in both phrases? Obviously, a son refers to a father. Thus, we say here that this "Son," who is both man and God, is the Son of the Father, who is God but in a way that does not exclude otherness within itself. But later on in the same passage, this same Son is identified as "Christ." This word means "the anointed one." He was the one awaited by the Jewish tradition. In the Gospel of John, we are told that this Son is called the "Word." This designation, more than any others, relates the Godhead to what we call philosophy. The same truth is thus expressed by saying that "the Word was made flesh and dwelt amongst us." This understanding meant that God was now within human history as Son of Man. Nothing could be quite the same after that presence among us.

We are told, recalling many different passages in Scripture, that the "Spirit" descended upon this Son. If he is a man, however, he needed a grounding in humanity. Men do not "see" spirits easily. But this man, as John said in his epistle, is touched with his own hands and seen with his own eyes. This Son's mother, as his conception, was told that the Holy Spirit would overshadow her. She was to call her Son Emmanuel, "God with us." And later, when he was baptized by John in the Jordan, this same Spirit descended on him. The same Father calls him "his Son, in whom he is well-pleased."

The Spirit is said to be sent by this Son after he departed this life, after he ascended. Indeed, he said that, unless he departed, the Spirit would not come. Moreover, when the Spirit did appear at Pentecost, he accustomed himself to this world. He now lived in this creation and among men. He was to be a spirit of truth so that all that was taught would be remembered. It was the Spirit who accomplished the Father's will. This "will" had something to do with men who had "grown old" in sin. Evidently this manifestation of sin was what occasioned the Father's new initiative, his sending the Son into the world so that the original purpose in creating them be not lost. So the whole narrative had something to do with sin, which had lasted a long time, long enough to see that men were not going to change much without some divine intervention.

Hence, men needed a "new life." This "new life," to be called "grace," was supplied by the Spirit. What did it entail? Obviously, it had something to do with sin; namely, its heinousness and its forgiveness. The first words of the Gospel were "repent," be converted, as if to say that this "new life" had a condition attached to it. What the Spirit had to give was not forced on sinners. God could receive into his life only those who freely responded to his mercy and love. It was up to them to accept what was offered to them after the manner of a gift. Indeed, one of the common names later given to the Spirit was precisely "Gift," as if to say that there is no compulsion in God's dealing with us, only a frank giving and explaining what is offered and why. The world and those of it can and often do refuse.

II

Though the word is not in Scripture, we call our God "Trinity." Islam, Judaism, and most religions and philosophies reject this understanding of God. It is said, wrongly, to mean that there are "three" gods. But it does not mean this. It is said to deny the oneness of God, even though it does not do this. Yet Christians recognize that they have to explain clearly why the seemingly obvious issue of the "three gods" is not their view. They also have to explain in a coherent manner why the fact of three Persons does not deny the oneness of the Godhead. How do they go about doing this?

First of all, the Christian understanding of God begins with and never denies the Jewish commandment that Yahweh is one God. There are no strange gods other than he. God is one. Though certain hints and intimations are found in the Old Testament that Wisdom and Spirit are in God— something similar in Aristotle—the notion of a single Creator, in whom heaven and earth find their origins, prevails. Thus, Christianity does not deny but affirms the truth of the oneness of the Hebrew understanding of God. But it leaves this one God open to further explanation of himself. This further explanation is what the New Testament is about.

But first, one thing from Aristotle had to be cleared up. Aristotle, in discussing friendship, had understood this highest virtue to be impossible within the Godhead, even though he acknowledged that God moved by will and knowledge. He was a "First Mover" who moved all else. But this God lacked something. He lacked friends. He lacked what seemed to be the highest of goods, the possibility of giving and sharing with others. Not a few philosophers, on this basis, wanted to hold that the world was created precisely so that God would not be lonely. But the revelation of Christ was based on two things. First, the world was not created because God lacked something. The world did not need to exist. God would be God whether it existed or not. Secondly, revelation teaches that within the one Godhead we find Father, Son, and Spirit, a trinity of persons. The Son, the Word, reflects everything that is the Father. The Father and the Son's bond pours forth in a Spirit a person who includes their union and difference. God is not lonely.

The word *trinity* was coined in order to explain how God was spoken of in the New Testament. The word itself was not scriptural, but what it meant was. There was no reason philosophical terms could not be used to understand what was taught. Thus, the Father sent the Son. The Father and the Son are one. He who knows the Son knows the Father. If we know the Son, we know the Father. The Son, after his resurrection, returned to the Father. But the Father and the Son send the Spirit to complete the work for which Christ, the Son, the Word, was sent into the world. The world did not accept him but crucified him. He died, was buried, but rose again. The life he received was the life that he had had with the Father from the beginning. He ascended into heaven, to the hand of the Father. Hence, he will return to judge the living and the dead. The Spirit will be with his people all days, even to the end of the world. The world will have an end, will pass away. We await a new heaven and a new earth.

The reason the world was created was not just to have a world. It was created for man. It was created to invite men to participate in the inner life of God, eternal life. This purpose had a twofold meaning. One was what man would do with or in the world once he appeared there. This is the actual turbulent history of man on this planet. The second was that each member of the human race was invited, from the beginning, to participate in the inner Trinitarian life of God. This invitation was something that was not possible unless a "new life" was infused into each person. Man was invited to be more than his nature was open to. This divine initiative was the purpose of the Redemption from the old sins.

God did not "need" the world. He did not need to create as if he needed something. This is why, from the human point of view, the Holy Spirit is described as a "gift." Not only is the world itself and all in it, including ourselves, a "gift" to us, so also is the effort of God to restore that disorder in the world that was put in it by human sin. In order to participate in this "gift" of "eternal life" offered to each of us, something had to be done about sin. And it had to be done in such a manner that the orders of creation be not overturned. Men remained what they are. What does that mean? It means, in dealing with the human rejection of his order in nature and grace, that God could not take away man's nature or freedom. He had to operate, as it were, with what he had created.

This restriction is what evidently surrounded the initiative of God to give man another way to reach him after the failure in Adam and Eve of his first effort. Adam and Eve had used their freedom to reject the initial offer of eternal life. They wanted to create their own way. All subsequent sin, in effect, imitates this claim. In doing so, the first couple suffered the consequences of their own choice. They were subject to death, as they were told. Their acts had consequences. If God the Son became man in the world, he could offer men another way. As it turns out, that the people to whom he was sent also rejected him. As a result, he died on the cross. It was this second effort of God to give us the gift of eternal life that we are left with in the Church until the end.

The Trinity indicates that God is, as it were, social in himself in such a way that he does not need anything. Creation is thus something rising out of love or generosity, not out of justice. But its purpose is serious. The rejection of the divine plan for each of us is a possible choice. This choice is what each human life is ultimately about. It always bears the character of "I will or will not serve." The primary purpose of God is the salvation of each of the persons he created in his image and likeness. It is not some apocalyptic inner-worldly political, economic, or ecological purpose down the ages.

The actual world is an arena in which the ultimate destiny of each person is worked out according to his own choices. Those who live in brutal societies are not further away from God's purpose for them than those who live in prosperous ones when it comes to the availability of eternal life. We are not supposed to create brutal societies, of course, even when we do. But people lose their souls both in good and bad societies. No one avoids the basic issue of how he stands in relation to sin and the redemption that God has offered.

The Trinity, then, is the way God has taught us to understand, as best we can, what he is like in his inner life to which we are invited. Like all invitations, we can refuse the invitation, the gift. But this inner life of the Godhead, Father, Son, and Spirit, is the only explanation for that unsettled sense in each of us that we are made for a purpose, a happiness. We cannot give what we really want to ourselves. But we can receive, if we will, as it has been offered to each of us. The precariousness of our world has its roots not in the fragility of our physical existence but in the temptation we all have to be ourselves the cause of our being, of our choosing on our own to "be like gods" as if God did not offer some understanding of himself far superior to anything we could imagine for ourselves.

CHAPTER 19

WELCOME, NUMBER 9,000,000,000!

IN 1977, I wrote a book entitled *Welcome, Number 4,000,000,000!* It was a sequel to *Human Dignity & Human Numbers* (1971). Both books dealt with the "population explosion," that era's supposed crisis issue. We were running out of resources of every kind. We would all be starving in a quarter of a century. Drastic policies for cutting down populations were proposed and often put into effect. Babies were *not* welcome. Everything was panic. The "green" movement began in this hectic atmosphere. "Save the earth, not the people!"

Such predictions of impending catastrophe were all wrong. Disaster did not occur. In "Apocalypse as a Secular Enterprise" (*The Scottish Journal of Theology,* 1976), I argued that this ecological frenzy grew, not from fact, but from a theological relocation of the transcendent order into this revolving world as man's ultimate and only destiny (see Schall, *The Modern Age*, 2011).

Moreover, as Julian Simon, Herman Kahn, and others at the time argued, because of certain key developments in growing grains, resources were available. The whole focus of these issues needed reorienting. The four billionth child was *not* a disaster. Its birth was rather a gift to be "welcomed." Why? It was precisely by having fresh brains and new demands that we learned to take care of ourselves, learned that the world is much richer than we understood. We now have seven billion people on this planet. They are generally better off than any previous generation in history. Why? We can and do learn how to deal with ourselves when we need to do so. The world, contrary to the pessimists, is not a parsimonious place unless, in our foolishness, we choose to make it that way. Some half-century after these population scares, however, Western civilization, by its own moral choices, experiences drastic population decline. Yet man's knowledge of everything about himself and his world has never been more developed.

Within the next fifty years or so, we are to expect a world population of nine billion inhabitants. Should we again push the panic button? These remarks are occasioned by a documentary I saw (July 21) on KQED San Francisco about world population. Initially, I thought that this analysis was a rehashed Paul Ehrlich, of *Population Bomb* fame. In a multi-scientist commentary, we did see graphs foretelling that world population will increase to nine or eleven billion in a few decades.

But this presentation was not in disaster-mode as so much environmentalism is. Rather, it argued that men do have the intelligence and capacity to deal with their increasing numbers. The documentary went through changes in agriculture, energy, and resources. We do have the capacity to deal with these things. George Gilder had long ago taught that wealth consists not primarily of material resources but brains.

What are we to make of this approach? First, environmentalism does have a totalitarian side. The papal advisor

Joachim Schellnhuber's solution is to reduce the world's population to less than a billion. Accomplishing this feat legitimizes vast programs of abortion, family control, euthanasia, and other such "necessary" steps. If we *a priori* maintain the impossibility of mankind to deal with its own needs as they arise, we must impose rigid control over all human activities and values.

What the TV documentary lacked was any interest in the purpose of man. Scientists know that the sun will burn out. Is man's purpose simply to keep himself afloat in space for as long as possible? What ultimately makes the difference, if resources are as limited as many claim, whether we use them up rapidly or gradually? In the end, the same number of people will be supported.

But if the world and its resources, human and natural, exist for a purpose other than just to float on and on, another end of man can be conceived. Our world is intended to end. It is a temporary place wherein we each work out our final transcendent goal. We have here no lasting city. Ecology wants to make it last by controlling numbers and activities.

A better way exists. The main reason why we may not be able to support everyone, especially the remaining poor, is not due to lack of resources or ways to support larger numbers of our kind with better human conditions. It is due to environmental and government theories that insist that we can do nothing but limit ourselves to a few privileged people and their limited offspring down the ages with no other purpose than keeping the earth afloat.

No reason exists why a population of nine billion cannot thrive. The purpose of our kind living on this planet is a transcendent one. The world will end when God chooses, probably with plenty of "resources" left over. Its end has little to do with caring for the planet but everything to do with how we live on it.

CHAPTER 20

THE "DECLARATION" OF VOLUNTARISM

We hold that any "law" of nature or polity can be other than it is.

Each human being is what he declares itself to be. No stable "human nature" exists apart from the individual citizen's definition of what he is.

Civil law is the only law human beings are not free to disobey, as it belongs to everyone. This limitation of personal freedom is the meaning of "common good" or "commonweal."

Society's purpose is to enable human beings to be whatever they chose to be, whatever it is.

No transcendent order exists to which any appeal against the civil law can be directed or justified.

The well-being of the planet Earth down the ages is more important than the lives of individual citizens at any time.

Human "rights" are determined and defined by civil law alone.

Religion has no objective validity; its customs and practices are subject to the civil law and must conform to it.

No organization or society stands between the individual citizen and the state.

No human being has a "right" to exist apart from the civil law's determination of when human life begins and ends or whether it is worth continued existence.

Children belong to whoever takes care of them. Civil society decides who is qualified to exercise this role.

The nature and constitution of a "family" is defined by the civil society.

The diversity of all members of any institution or society recognized by the civil society is to reflect the diversity of the citizens. A society not recognized by the state has no standing.

"Truth" is not a category recognized by civil society. No contradiction between truth and civil society is possible. "Truth" is what civil society decides it is.

Whatever the civil society wills is the law.

Freedom, both individual and societal, is conditioned by what the civil society decides. The will to be "free" means the will to obey the law, whatever it is.

"Science" does not run against civil law. In a conflict between science and civil law, civil law decides.

Human equality means obedience to the way the law treats individual citizens.

What is law in one time or place can be its opposite in another time and place.

Marriage is a civil contract with no intrinsic relation to children. The education of children is the sole responsibility of civil society and whom it designates.

The adult members of a "family" can be composed of any combination of sex, gender, or other form of diversity.

No transcendent judgment about final punishment or reward for human conduct exists.

The purpose of civil society is to provide for the health, the material, and cultural well-being of its citizens through its own agencies and defined by its own norms.

The words and language of citizens are subject to state surveillance. "Hate-language" is to be defined and punished by civil law.

Citizens are free to do what they want provided it does not infringe on what others want to do. It is the function of civil society to define what infringes on the freedom of others.

The Socratic principle that it is "never right to do wrong" is incoherent.

Every citizen has a "right" not merely to pursue happiness but to be happy. It is the function of the state to guarantee and bring this right to its completion.

Freedom is unrelated to property or purpose.

Good government requires citizens who freely obey the law, whatever it is.

The terms *god, logos, trinity, incarnation,* and *redemption* are incoherent and have no legal standing. They are unrelated to anything in reality.

Virtue is a habit whereby we are able to do what we want to do, whatever it is.

No independent order of reason exists. Reason is the capacity that enables us to achieve what we want more easily.

The distinction of the sexes has no purpose or foundation.

Abortion and euthanasia are guaranteed "rights" because, without them, citizens would not be free to define their own lives.

The cosmos has no intrinsic purpose. Its order is arbitrary and by chance. It has no origin in "mind" or "intelligence." The only intelligence in the universe belongs to men. It enables them to impose their own "values" on the world. These "values" change according to the desires of human beings.

Human beings are not exceptions to the arbitrariness of the cosmos. They are free because they have no internal or external order to direct them.

Education deals with ideas. Ideas contradict each other. Education for freedom means understanding the intrinsic nature of ideas. A "liberal" education is one that frees us from any claim to truth.

Revelation of a "god" from outside the cosmos cannot happen. Nothing exists outside the cosmos. Anything "revealed" could be "otherwise." Hence, it would be indistinguishable from what exists that can also be otherwise.

CHAPTER 21

ON FOOLS

"WHAT fools these mortals be!" is an oft-cited passage from Shakespeare's *Midsummer Night's Dream*. In my memory, I recall it to read: "What fools *we* morals be," as if it were spoken by one of our kind who looks back at man's checkered record of living on this earth. But the passage is, rather, spoken by Puck, a sprite, an observer not of our lineage. Something non-human sees our real situation. To me, this Shakespearean passage always contained a warmth about it—"A what-else-would-you-expect of this odd lot we call humanity?" The myriads of foibles, yes sins, of our kind were not, *ipso facto*, a reason why we should not exist. Surely someone must enjoy seeing how it all plays out. If the sheep were not lost, the "more joy in heaven" could not have happened.

In our literature, fools, such as court jesters or comedians, are often poignant characters. Men who make us laugh frequently lead rather sad lives—I think of Durante, Bert Lahr, the Marx Brothers, even Benny. At Comedy Central, which I seldom find funny, I often seem to see desperate men and women doing their level best to pretend to themselves that the world is not something other than one big joke. Yet, not surprisingly, really funny stories, incidents, yarns, parodies, and self-descriptions are found almost everywhere. What would our lives be without them? Any comedian, probably any human being, has at some point to see himself or allow others to see him as a fool.

Scripture does not give fools much of a break. We are not supposed to call anyone a fool (Mt 5:22). It is the fool who claims, "There is no God" (Ps 14:1). Whether all those who make this "no god" claim are fools can be debated. Paul tells the Corinthians that what philosophers teach is often pretty foolish. He even tells us that "the foolishness of God is wiser than the thoughts of men." Meanwhile, the Gentiles think that the teaching of Christ crucified is a bit "foolish." The Second Psalm tells us, "He who sits in the heavens laughs" at those who rage against the Lord (v. 4).

Any number of studies are grouped around the paradoxical notion of "Christ the Fool." The point of such considerations is that Christ looked so odd to the world that he will always be taken for a madman or a fool. His own relatives seem to have thought this way. When confronted with the possibility that Christ really was what he said he was, we are left with little leeway. Either he was a fool or he was the Messiah. If the latter be the case, the term has a whole new meaning to us when he is called foolish.

In another sense, however, foolishness stands for a certain lightsomeness about our place in the world. Not all things are serious. Not all serious things are solemn. Almost every solemn occasion can cause an incident of laughter when something goes wrong. When we finally see the point of a joke, its reasons, when we finally succeed in "getting it," our reaction is a sense of elation. Paul talked about the delight of those who ran the race. No joy can be found in an inert existence.

In a sequence entitled "Charlie Brown on Self-Respect," Charlie sits alone on a playground bench. He says to himself forlornly, "I always have to have lunch alone," but adds, "I'd sure like to have lunch with that little red-haired girl." He gets a foolish idea. "I wonder if I walked over and asked her to have lunch with me. . . ." But, to himself, he figures, "She'll probably laugh right in my face." Still by himself, he concludes poignantly, "It's hard on a face when it gets laughed at."

Is there such a thing as a fool? I suppose we could say, "Why, I meet one or two every day!" We know that others meet us. We wonder if they think us fools. And if so, do they have grounds for so thinking? Too often they do.

I recall a ballad that contained the refrain "I'm a fool, I know, for loving you. . . ." Loving famously brings out odd things in lovers. The world is amused (or at least was) by moonstruck lads suddenly acting in an erratic manner on meeting "the right young lady." "Lovers' quarrels" should best end in a laughter that, on working things out, is the result of recognizing in oneself some foolishness or other.

But the paradoxical image of "Christ the Fool" still haunts. It was the Man who was thought a fool even by wise professors, clerics, and his own relatives who redeemed us. Why did they taunt him as foolish? I suppose because they could not imagine anything better than they had. The Divine Fool could.

CHAPTER 22

TWO TRUTHS REVISITED

CONSIDERABLE turmoil has been generated by a tweet from a Vatican-related Twitter account. It proposed that two plus two in science equals four but in theology the sum could equal five. This "possibility" of five was not exactly new or even startling, except perhaps for its source. The two-truth theory has its uses, no doubt. Machiavelli famously proposed that human freedom would be exponentially expanded if at least the prince rid himself of the distinction between good and evil. In effect, he proposed a version of this theory that is usually associated with the Muslim thinkers Averroes and Al-Ghazali. The "truth" of politics and the "truth" of morality are both true. We affirm that evil should not be done. But sometimes it should be done. In that case, it becomes good by being evil.

The two-truth theory held, in its purest form, that a truth of reason and a truth of religion or theology could contradict each other. But both still are true. The Aristotelian tradition held that this situation could not be the case. One view was right; the other was wrong. Reason cannot contradict reason, be it human or divine. That is what reason means. A thing cannot be and not be at the same time in the same circumstances. This is called a "first principle." It is so called because nothing can be clearer from which to deduce the principle. We affirm that something exists. At the same time, we implicitly deny that it is.

The average man may not be carried away by these seemingly esoteric reflections. In truth they are quite fascinating. Some ancient Greeks and Romans dickered with such thoughts, as did later the followers of Occam. The people who, on a large scale, first utilized the proposition that a truth of reason and a truth of theology could contradict each other were seeking to defend Allah. Why did Allah need defending? It was because of a book he is said to have written manifesting his mind. The men who developed these notions were pious men. They were sharp enough to see that, in a book said to be revealed, contradictory claims were made. Something had to be done to cover the reputation of the god against evident inconsistencies.

The solution such thinkers came up with, when spelled out, was remarkable. They did not deny that contradictions existed. They said that Allah could will one thing on Tuesday and its opposite on Wednesday. The latest affirmation is always the binding one but it can change tomorrow. In thinking these notions through, things became ever more complicated.

If the will of Allah could affirm one thing on Tuesday and its opposite on Wednesday, he could do the same thing with all the laws of nature. Since truth is not grounded in *logos*, but in *voluntas*—that is, the will—the only way we could know that the sun will arise in the morning is if God wills it and we believe it. He could will that it not come up. These presuppositions mean that we cannot really rely on "nature" for anything.

Nobody but Allah does anything. It is blasphemy to suggest otherwise. If we make a fortune one day but lose it the next, in both cases it is the will of Allah. Our enterprise has nothing to do with it. Our skills or lack thereof mean nothing. Science cannot really exist in such a world. No incentive is found to investigate "nature" if it can be otherwise at every instant.

A sort of hybrid Christian-secularist version of this theory exists, particularly in moral and political philosophy. Nature is evaporated of any content. The difference between Islam and this Western view is not so great when we come right down to it. One theory makes Allah's will responsible for what goes on so that whatever happens is Allah's will. The other theory places the will in the individual person so that he is not subject to any ordered nature but only to his own will. The Machiavellian version is simply "What the prince (democracy) wills is the law," to cite a Roman law adage cited by Aquinas. In a conflict of individual and collective will, the latter almost always wins, as Hobbes saw.

Why are two-truth theories proposed? Almost invariably they arise to justify what cannot be justified in reason, including the reason of faith. When some position, said to belong to revelation, can only be justified by denying that the Divinity is bound by reason, by *logos*, we know we are dealing with the two-truth issue. Ultimately, the justification of "heresy" always involves, in its logic, the denial of reason. Or to put it the other way around, when we see that what is called "revelation" needs to resort to arbitrary will, divine or human, to justify itself, we know that we have reached incoherence.

CHAPTER 23

WHAT IS POLITICAL PRUDENCE?

THE first name of a Mexican man I know is *Prudencio*. In Victorian novels, young ladies were often named "Prudence." The most important virtue that a statesman can possess is prudence, combined with magnanimity. The word itself, however, has come to mean overly cautious, unwillingness to try something new. But in its classical sense, prudence meant the ability to see workable alternatives that still kept on track for achieving human well-being from which prudence takes its initial direction.

Prudence is the intellectual virtue of the moral virtues—courage, temperance, justice, and prudence. It deals principally with means to ends. What does that mean? It means that if I am the head of the Mafia, I must judge the means that enable me to control all the illegal dealings in Chicago. The "prudent" Capo can best figure out how it all works by keeping the law at bay while collecting protection monies. This example emphasizes that "prudence" does not itself choose the end of our lives. It deliberates and decides the means whereby the purpose we have selected, good or bad, may "reasonably" be achieved.

Prudence is an acquired habit. We are not born with it, just as we are not born with courage or temperance. We have to acquire prudence by practice; that is, by making particular prudent decisions. Prudence is not a "theoretical"

virtue, not a virtue only concerned with the truth of something. Prudence is concerned with the truth as it appears in
things being put into effect for a right (or wrong) reason.
One does not have to know the definition of prudence to
be prudent in action. The famous Latin definition of prudence is *recta ratio agibilium*—right reasoning in things to
be done or put into effect. Prudence means, in other words,
that what we do in our relations with ourselves and others, including our political relations, is to put order into
our actions, institutions, and laws. These are the things for
which we are praised or blamed. The only way things are
going to be ordered is if we deliberately put order there.
The primary object of prudence is our own good order. We
are the beings in the universe whose own personal well-
being is up to them. We can thus choose to be or not to be
prudent.

Why think about these things? Prudence is different
from but akin to art or craft. In art, the object of our rule is
not ourselves but the thing to be made or crafted. Art is the
skill whereby we manage to put into some external object,
a piece of wood or stone, the configuration we want. Art
does not look to the goodness or badness of the artist but
to the object to be made. A good artist, Aristotle said, can
show someone what it means to make something badly. In
doing so, he does not become a bad man. But if a politician
thinks he is primarily a man of art not prudence, he will
assume that he can use evil means to reach a good end.
Substantially, this latter position was that of Machiavelli
and of Callicles in Plato. The confusion of art and politics
has serious political consequences.

What is the goal of a "prudent" politician? It is not simply "success" in achieving what he wants, whatever it is. The prudent politician is concerned with a "common good." What does that mean? It does not mean some grandiose idea that he seeks to impose on his polity to make it holy or perfect. Rather, it means guiding actions, institutions, and laws in such a fashion that the particular good of each citizen can be attained by his own, not the politician's actions. This is why a politician's life, like that of a parent, is at bottom sacrificial. That is, it looks not to his glory but to the good of others.

Many writers have remarked that the one person whom we least want as a political official is the one who desires the job. If someone "wants" the office too much, he is probably not looking to the good of others. In most polities, politicians manage to be pretty well compensated compared to the normal run of men. The contrast between their interest and the interest of the public is a well-known theme in political life.

Prudence, to repeat, is the intellectual virtue of the moral virtues. It is the virtue of the statesman who is properly ordered to what is good in human life and in his polity. It means, however, the ability to see, in the myriad of practical alternatives available to him, what avenue really does reach that common good whereby individual citizens in their own lives can, in their own prudence, reach the given purpose for which they exist.

CHAPTER 24

WHAT AM I?

IN a newspaper, I once saw the following headlines: The first announced that some professor held that apes have "human rights." Other professors think that trees have "rights" of some sort. The second headline maintained that some, but not all, human fetuses are protected by law. If you are a negligent driver and kill a pregnant lady in a crash, that fetus in her womb is human. You can be sued. But other unborn babies are not human. You get in big trouble by thinking they are. The final headline reported that most Americans do not believe that the devil is real.

If I ever had any doubts about the existence of Old Nick, such reasoning as the ones displayed in these headlines would make me pretty sure that most Americans, on this latter score, are quite wrong. No human culture by its own unaided thinking could be so confused in its logic about good order if there were not some spiritual power confusing it at a very deep level. Moreover, not to give the devil all the credit, if not to prove his existence, such contradictory intellectual positions could not come about apart from our own choosing. The devil is not so strong that he can actually make us hold what we do not, for our own reasons, choose to hold.

The German philosopher Heidegger, I believe, speaks of our experience of having been "thrown" into existence.

Some theories of evolution affirm that we were first thrown into being as apes or dolphins or some such creature. But it is dangerous to speak this way. We then want to ask, "Well, who threw us into this existence that we did not choose by ourselves?" Surely not even an ape could imagine a human being throwing himself into existence. If we find ourselves already to be human beings, not apes or trees, we can distinguish ourselves from either.

The humorist Will Cuppy once wrote a book entitled *How to Tell Your Friends from the Apes*. But, as far as we can tell, no ape ever wondered to himself, "Why am I not a human being?" One cannot but be amused by the image of some ape solemnly wondering about his "human rights," or better, wondering if human beings have "ape rights." A smart ape, looking over the human record, would probably not choose to become human. Will law schools begin to have courses on "ape rights" as a special branch of "human rights?" Actually, animal "rights" courses are common in major law schools today. Still, it takes a human being to wonder why he is or is not an ape. Indeed, it takes a human being to consider why he is not essentially different from an ape. Apes, bless them, don't think this way. Some animals obviously can figure some things that they need out. No ape ever wrote a document beginning "All apes are created equal with certain inalienable rights . . ."

Eric Voegelin remarked that our first existential question is "What is the ground of my being?" It is impossible to think that I cause myself to be what I already am. Most of us have some evidence, reported by our relatives, that once we did not exist. We were not even imagined by anyone we know personally. Yet I do stand outside of nothingness as a certain kind of being. I not only can ask questions, but I expect to find answers. We assume that an answer exists to the question of why we exist as individuals and as human beings, not apes. Albert Camus remarked that the first philosophic question is "Why do I not commit suicide?" The answer must be that, however I explain it, something is to be preferred to suicide. That something is human life and its drama.

What am I? The classic answer to that question is that we are "substances of a rational nature." We realize that we are, while being "whats," also "whos." That is to say, we are beings who are "called." We are spoken to. We can listen, hear. Our rational nature is also social. We are not complete by ourselves, however much we really have our own selves. We are not, cannot be, and do not want to be, someone else.

Aristotle had already made this same point. No one would want to have all the goods of the world, he thought, on the condition of being someone else. A pessimist might say, "We are stuck with ourselves." On the other hand, something about us needs completion in someone else. Philosophers and theologians say that even if we are made for ourselves, we are made for others. Indeed, we are made to love. "To love" means literally that by remaining myself, I foster the real good of someone else and the other fosters mine. Friendship means that someone else is concerned with my particular good for its own sake.

Thomas Aquinas, when he came to explain how we might understand our relation to God, explained it, following the Apostle John, in terms of friendship. That is, God was concerned for our good. But Aquinas did not think that we actually became gods. We remained ourselves, which is what we prefer to do, even before God. Ultimately, this remaining ourselves is what the resurrection of the body is about. Of course, we also want God to be God. We really do not want to remake him in our own dull images, though we are created in his image. If I am a *what* that is also a *who*, it must mean that any "who" can relate itself to me. If God is also a "who," as seems to be the case, then what I am will find its meaning in a kind of anticipation or expectation. God is revealed as three Persons who can address all persons and hear them in return.

What if I, as a good American, do not believe that the devil exists? C. S. Lewis remarked, in his *Screwtape Letters,* that the best the devil, as a rational, scheming being, could hope for would be that human beings did not believe he existed. Then it might be possible, as Lewis pointed out elsewhere, to "abolish" man, that hated thing that God had created. What would this "abolishing" look like? It would, I think, look pretty much like what we are busy doing in our labs, courts, legislatures, presidential decrees, and seminars. We are trying to clone ourselves, artificially beget ourselves, confuse ourselves with apes, eliminate those of ourselves we do not want, abolish the family, all in the name of "improving" our well-being.

Aquinas, in his treatise on charity, observed that "properly speaking, man is not human, but superhuman." He implied by this that if we did not understand the prime destiny to which we are called by our being thrown into existence, we would end up not with what is human but with what is less than human. That is to say, apes have "human rights." If it were not so dangerous, we could almost laugh at the ridiculousness of it all. They say the devil does laugh, a terrible laughter.

What indeed am I? We are also beings, as Aristotle said, who can laugh, laugh at the silliness of our own often-terrible theories, theories that we see become practice before our very eyes. In not freely accepting what we are, we see ourselves choosing to become what we ought not to be. This is the meaning of our times.

What am I? Evidently, I am also a being who can choose to rid myself of those things in myself that most constitute my dignity and my destiny. I am a being who can define my own freedom as something presupposed to nothing, to no *what-I-am*. With this radical freedom, I can claim that what I am is totally dependent on what I choose myself to be. This result was approximately what the account of the Fall in Genesis was about.

The only thing a rational "who" that wants to retain the original human idea can do in this situation is to recall *what-it-is-to-be-a-human-being*. In this light, he can see that that into which we choose to refashion ourselves is an inverse or perverse image of what it is we were before we began to tamper with our being. Ironically, we have become a people who do not believe in the devil. Our ancestors who burned a few witches at Salem did believe in the devil. We think them barbarous. We do not think ourselves barbarous. We think of ourselves as creating a "new man." We no longer understand the kind of being that was thrown into being in the first place. We are left alone with ourselves. No ape has any idea of the loneliness we have chosen for ourselves. If we cannot imagine it, perhaps the only "rights" we deserve are, after all, "animal rights," defined not by the way we ought to live but by the way the animals do live.

CHAPTER 25

WHAT EXACTLY IS EASTER?

I

A S a general principle, an honest man will want to know what something is or is said to be before he decides whether he thinks it is true or that he must do anything about it. Take one's relation to a doctor. Insofar as we deal with a doctor *qua* doctor, we want him to tell us the truth about what is wrong with us. If we didn't, we should not bother him. We do not, if we are normal, want him to lie to us. Unless we know what the problem is, we cannot decide what, if anything, we need to do about it. And if we decide the doctor is incompetent, we still have to find one that is.

Definitions are good things. They are intended to tell us what a thing is in words we understand. Generally, we want to know what a thing is whether we like it or not. Indeed, we need to know what things can harm us and which ones help us. We understand that it is dangerous for us deliberately to choose not to know the truth about something. On the basis of what they are and of what we are, our knowledge relates us to everything that is not ourselves.

In the Easter season, someone who does not know much about what it means might well ask, "What exactly is Easter anyhow?" Accurate knowledge of it is not always easy to come by. Indeed, we have the impression that many people do not want to know what it really is lest it make a demand on them that they are not willing to consider. Still, what would be a fair and accurate answer to an honest inquiry about Easter, one that had no further purpose but to hear accurately what this word and the reality to which it refers mean? On hearing the explication, the inquiring listener might say, "So that is what it means!" or, "Makes no sense to me!" or, "I had it all wrong," or, "It's really complicated," or, "Run that by me again." In any case, the question—"What is Easter?"—is a worthy one.

II

The word *Easter* can have several origins—an Anglo-Saxon goddess of Spring, a Frankish way of referring to the east and the rising sun, a reference to the Jewish Passover. For Christians and anyone who wants to know about its meaning, it recalls the day on which Christ rose from the dead. Each of the three words—*Christ, rose, dead*—refer to a specific reality.

Taken in itself, "Christ rose from the dead" is a straight-forward statement of what Easter means, of what it is to which the sentence refers. Spelled out, it recalls that a young Jewish man, called Christ, claimed to be the Son of God. He was executed in Jerusalem under Roman authority about thirty years after his birth in Bethlehem. Contemporary witnesses maintained that three days after his execution on a cross, he rose again from the dead. The same witnesses initially had a hard time believing this event, but they also had more difficulty in denying what they saw and touched. So they concluded that it was a fact that they witnessed.

"To rise again" means that the same individual, who was actually dead, reappeared, identified himself as the same person who died, though in a transfigured manner. Dead means what dead means. Life had ceased in him. Once we understand what Easter means, we are not asked to accept this unexpected truth as if it had no justification. No one denies that most dead men stay dead. Even the two dead men whom this Christ was said to have brought back to life, the widow's son and Lazarus, subsequently died. This did not happen to Christ.

Throughout subsequent history, many efforts have been made to explain how this event and its testimony could not be true. These efforts have their value. Each time this Resurrection is denied, something new about its reality comes to be understood. Muslims, for example, maintain that God cannot suffer. Therefore, Christ was not God and was not crucified. Some Jews just after Christ's death were worried that the disciples would claim that he rose again, as he said he would, so they paid some soldiers to testify that the body was carried away at night. Therefore, the disciples only pretended that it rose again.

Many different theories were subsequently developed to explain what happened as if the Resurrection did not or could not have happened. It is a difficult reality, so we can expect many efforts to insist either that Christ did not rise again or that he really did not exist in the first place. The disciples were said to have "wanted" Christ to rise so badly that they "imagined" that he did. But the record shows that the actual disciples themselves were, to put it mildly, "slow to believe," as well they might have been.

The disciples were not finally convinced by their imagination but by the facts of what they saw and heard. We can, of course, maintain that they were ignorant fishermen, so what did they know? But it is more likely that these supposedly ignorant fishermen, who were used to catching and cutting up fish, were quite well aware that what they saw went against all common experience. They just knew that it happened. They did not deny their experience under pressure. Only later did they and their followers come to reflect on how and why it could have happened in terms that kept the truth of what they saw intact but did not at the same time contradict reality.

III

Let's then grant that we understand what is meant by Easter, by the Resurrection. One does not have to be a believer to understand what is being said. That is precisely what anyone who wants to know the meaning of things would want to know. But so what? Does it make any real difference? Why not just let this information go at that? We do not have to worry our heads about it.

That would be a perfectly reasonable position if the Resurrection of Christ was intended to include himself alone. All along, this Man who rose again kept insisting that what happened to him would happen to everyone else who bore the same human nature that he assumed. Now for anyone who has ever thought of the end of his own life, whether it just ends in death, this Resurrection is a pretty consoling doctrine. It means that our lives do not end when they end in death. It looks more like they really begin when they end in death.

One further hitch arises. It seems that our lives are not just an uneventful unrolling of the number of years during which we were alive. Different people live different kinds of lives. Some lasted longer than others. Many never really got much of a start. Quite a few never made it out of the womb. The resurrection of the body connoted the putting back together of what belonged together. Death, in act, may not have been intended from the beginning. And if this Christ was really the Son of God, as he claimed, what was he doing becoming man? The usual answer to this recurring question is that he wanted to save sinners.

It takes a while for that idea of saving sinners to sink in, especially since it was affirmed that Christ himself was sinless. He did not have to become other than he was within the Godhead. It seems that the One that he called his Father asked him to take on human nature. He was obedient and accepted whatever followed. What followed in the end was pretty gory. The Roman method of executing criminals was devised to be as cruel as possible.

IV

Again, all of this seems odd. Why would God have to go through this convoluted way just to redeem sinners? Why not just a word and be done with it? Were the dalliances, bickerings, and betrayals that men imposed on each other so bad? Evidently, the Father thought them so. Christ maintained that, in the end, every mortal person would follow his path to resurrection of the body. The whole person would be restored. Every person was initially intended for eternal life, not just for a few years in what came to be called, in a graphic expression, a "vale of tears."

Good philosophers tell us that the world need not have existed at all. If the world did not need to exist, it follows that none of us ever needed to exist either. But the fact is that both the world and we ourselves in it do exist, though we seem pretty finite and fragile. This consideration pushes the question back to the Father again. If he did not "need" these creatures of his creation that seemed so frequently to wander off the reservation, why bother with them? Obviously, it was not just so that he would have something to do to keep busy.

It seems, when all the fog has cleared away, that the Father wanted to invite each of the creatures who knew he was mortal into the inner life that he shared with the Son and Spirit, the Persons of his own one life. It turns out that the world was not something that needed to happen, but something that was chosen to happen in order that, within it, human persons could be invited home, to a place in which they did not belong but into which they could be invited.

But like any invitation, the one invited needs to accept the invitation. If he is forced to accept it, he is not really invited in any proper sense. Moreover, any invitation can be turned down. Why is this possibility of turning an invitation down important? It is because the life within the Godhead into which we are invited can include only those who want to be there, who want to share the life that is already there. Any rejection of the invitation is self-chosen. The consequences that follow are not indifferent or inconsequential. The one who rejects the invitation is left with himself as the alternative to a life of participation within the Godhead. In effect, on the basis of the invitation, the world is divided into two cities, as Augustine said.

When we set out to inquire about what the Resurrection of Christ is, it turns out to include an inquiry into the question of what we ourselves are. We do not really have the choice of becoming nothing. Since we are immortal and ordered to resurrection, our most fundamental choice is to accept or reject an invitation to be more than we are by our given nature. We did not, in fact, have a choice about whether we would exist or not in the first place. It is impossible to imagine being given a choice to exist before we exist.

Existence was given to each of us, and it was good that we exist. We find ourselves already in existence. We are invited to accept what we are or to reject it. If we reject it, we are allowed to live with this rejection as what forms our being for the rest of eternity. This consequence is but another way of affirming how important our lives really are. Christ, the Son of God, rose from the dead. In that brief sentence, if we look carefully enough, we can discover the whole order of being and our place within it.

CHAPTER 26

DE ANIMALI AMBULANTE

"We walk the same block as dogs yet see different things. We walk alongside rats though each of us lives in the dusk of the other. We walk alongside other people and do not see what each of us knows, what each of us is doing—captured instead by the inside of our own heads."
—Alexandra Horowitz, *On Looking: A Walker's Guide to the Art of Observation.*[7]

I

SEVERAL years ago, knowing my proclivities, Anne Burleigh, for Christmas, gave me Alexandra Horowitz's book on walking and looking or looking while walking. I have written a number of books that, in some sense, can be called "walking books"—*Idylls & Rambles, The Sum Total of Human Happiness,* and *The Classical Moment.* But for me, the great introduction to walking is found in the essays of Belloc. Of course, Belloc was also a sailor, as his *Cruise of the Nona* reminds us. But sailing is nothing else but a continuation of walking, only on water with the help of a boat. I tried to capture some of this almost mystical

---

[7] Alexandra Horowitz, *On Looking: A Walker's Guide to the Art of Observation* (New York: Scribner 2011), 263.

sense of how walking looks into everything in my book
Remembering Belloc.

Somewhere, I remember reading a story about a couple—they might have been English—who had made some
sort of vow to walk the streets of the great and not so great
cities on every continent of the world. They did not seem
to have written any journal or reflections about what they
saw. Somehow that bothered me, that walking without seeing, or, at least, not telling us what was seen. Yet, as C.
S. Lewis said, if we tried to record everything that happened to us and about us in strict detail during any twen-
ty-four hour period of our lives, we would fill volumes and
volumes leaving little time for the events of another day.
Only if we do not see or hear everything can we see and
hear something. For us, the reality of everything can only
begin with the reality of a something. This human inability
to name everything is probably one of the proofs for the
divine existence. When it is due to lack of time, we call it
eternity.

So it was with some pleasure that I read this charming
book of Alexandra Horowitz. I must confess, though, that
I am not much of a dog lover. When walking in strange
parts, I follow that sage advice attributed to Theodore Roo-
sevelt for politicians to "walk softly but carry a big stick." I
learned from sad experience that when an owner of a bark-
ing hound says in a friendly voice, "Oh, my Fido does not
bite!" to be prepared for action. A large, long walking stick
is as good as an atom bomb when it comes to deterring
hungry bulldogs who confuse your left leg with their daily
portion of Purina Chow. Though they are reputed to be
man's best friend, and may well be, I prefer them out in

the wild somewhere hunting rabbits or being hunted by bears. "Love me, love my dog" I have always considered an immoral aphorism, though, I confess, you lose a lot of friends questioning its worthiness.

So it was also with some trepidation when I read that Horowitz "teaches animal behavior, and canine cognition at Barnard College." I always wondered what the young ladies studied there. She has a previous book entitled *Inside of a Dog: What Dogs See, Smell, and Know*. My confidence in the special status of mankind among the other denizens of this earth was considerably reassured when I learned that only human beings took this aforementioned course at Barnard. Although I do recall the story of some students at the University of California at Berkeley, I think, who, to prove a point about the nature of bureaucracy, registered a dog as a freshman, went to all his classes, wrote all his papers, and saw him graduate *cum laude* four years later. That is one dog that I should have enjoyed meeting without my usual walking stick.

II

On Looking is indeed about walking, walking in cities, especially in New York, though we see Philadelphia also. Indeed, this is a teaching book. We do not have to move to Manhattan, where Horowitz lives, to practice what she preaches, which is basically that much is to be seen on your very own block, your very own street. In some ten accounts of walking around a single city block, often beginning from her own front door, Horowitz circles, or squares, or rectangles a city block. On each turn around the block, she is accompanied by someone else who teaches her by example, word, or gesture what to see that she might have otherwise missed. Horowitz begins by walking with her little toddler son. What is it that little kids see and hear? If you walk around a city block with a child and let him look at or walk over to what interests him, you will see all sorts of things that you otherwise would have missed. "A 'walk', according to my toddler, is regularly about not walking. It has nothing to do with points A, B, or the getting from one to the other. It barely has anything to do with planting one's feet in a straight line. A walk is instead an investigatory exercise that begins with energy and ends when (and only when) exhausted" (21). This passage reminds me of an article I once read about a highly trained and conditioned athlete who submitted himself to an experiment. He was required to stay with a very young child and imitate every motion that the child made with his hands, legs, head, and body. It turned out the athlete was completely "pooped out," as they say, before the day was half over.

Horowitz is very systematic. She walks with a blind lady who taps her way around the block, who hears when an awning is over her head as she passes under it. Horowitz walks with a man who is a specialist in rocks and geology. She ends up realizing that the rocks, cement, and stones she walks over or around every day come from quarries all over New England, even Italy. They go back thousands and millions of years to reveal the remnants of ancient shellfish. She then walks with a doctor and next with a physical therapist. Just by looking at the gait of an old man, or the complexion of a lady, or speed of other walkers that they meet, one notices people who need a hip replacement or display other disorders.

Horowitz manages to find a gentleman who specializes in bugs. If we take a walk around the block on Manhattan, of all places, we find slugs, lady bugs, beetles, various leaf insects, worms, cockroaches, heaven knows what. She tells of a man who wrote a paper about the many different kinds of ants found in a mile of a New York street. Too, many kinds of animals besides the human variety are found on the island. Rats (the rodent kind) seem to enjoy living and flourishing among men. Even raccoons are prevalent. While no bears or mountain lions have been sighted in recent decades, evidently coyotes have been spotted, and if not in Manhattan, certainly in other cities, numberless protected deer enjoy dining on the local flowers and plants.

So with other companions, Horowitz goes into private public places like homes for the aged. She does not do any shopping on these jaunts, but windows are noticed. They do go into one church. They notice the flow of traffic and the walkers, especially the more recent menace of cell-phone users who are prone to bump into trees and other pedestrians. The busy cell-phoners have taken the place of the man who walked down the street reading a newspaper or book.

I particularly enjoyed the chapter on sounds that we hear outside in streets. Horowitz cites the composer John Cage. I recall being struck with Cage's book *Silence*, in which he noted that there is really no such thing as silence. There are always sounds of one form or another, including the sounds within our own bodies. Doctors listen to our internal sounds with stethoscopes or other listening devices. The last chapter was on the smells of the city, a walk with her dog. We all know about K-9 Corps and drug sniffing dogs. But a city is filled with all sorts of things, bugs, rocks, plants, sounds, smells, sights, things to touch and feel with our hands or wind on our cheeks and the sound of rain on an umbrella, or the smell of a lawn after a rain. The sense of smell is probably more important than we realize. Much of our eating has more to do with smell than taste. We identify people with certain smells. Smell seems instantaneous. Like the sound of a voice, smell can transcend time. A certain perfume will remind us of our grandmother if we catch it on someone else later in life. The unforgettable stench of my uncle's hog lot, now long turned into a corn field, comes back when I happen to run across hogs in some farm lot.

When we look at what Horowitz has done in this very good book, it is to go through our five senses. Sometimes I had the impression that Horowitz thought it was our brain that knew instead of we ourselves knowing in the way we do because our souls are forms of bodies with highly organized parts. It reminds me of the chapters in Leon Kass's book *The Hungry Soul,* in which he explains why each sense organ—eye, nose, ears, mouth—is placed where it is precisely so that we do know that which is not ourselves in all its details. Reflecting on the book, I kept thinking of the passage in Psalms 94: "He who planted the ear hear, does he not hear? / He who formed the eye, does he not see?" (v. 9). A walk around a city block should also, I think, cause us to wonder why we see, hear, smell, taste, or think at all.

The walk, alas, did not include stops at local New York delis. Horowitz did not walk around the block with her local rabbi. New York in many ways is a Jewish city. A rabbi would easily recall the songs, the smells, the bricks, the sounds of the Hebrew Bible as they walked these streets. Nor did she walk with a policeman or fireman. With each, she could have looked at the locks, bars of windows, alarms, emergency phones, as well as being mindful of the darker side of human existence. Amusingly, she does mention the fire hydrants, but these mostly in the context of dogs.

Each of these possible companions, plus numerous others, I am sure Alexandra Horowitz knows and realizes that her rounds could always add a new nuance to her seeing. But she accomplishes her purpose with the walks that she does take. It is simply that there is so much to know in the very place that we are that we have, probably not just from "evolution," the coordinated mind and senses whereby we can know what we encounter about us.

In the end, what we are left with is simply the delight of knowing, indeed, of being taught or reminded of an ever-new way to know what we think we already know. This "Walker's Guide to the Art of Observation" is, I think, a happy treatise on what it entitles itself, "On Looking"—and also on smelling, touching, tasting, and hearing, on bodies endowed with senses and minds that enable each of us to know that we know, know that smelling is not hearing, that observing is not tasting, that seeing is also believing. For it is we ourselves who see and look and wonder at *what is*, even on a given block in New York City where we happen to live.

CHAPTER 27

ON THE WORD *RELIGION*

W E know, hopefully, that the First Amendment talks of neither "establishing" a religion nor preventing its "free" exercise. Such legal language is not exactly the same as "freedom of religion" or the more recent freedom "from" religion. We also know that precisely defining "religion" can be a dicey matter. We now talk of atheists being protected by the First Amendment as if their "sect" were a "religion-less" religion. Amusingly, were there no God, we could not talk of an "a-theist." That very word is simply the Greek way to deny a subject already known.

We may possibly have heard of a difference between revealed and natural religions. Many universities have classes in the "philosophy" of religion, fewer on the "religion" of philosophy. Some scholars tell us that over twenty thousand Protestant sects can be distinguished. By now, most people are aware of the Sunni and Shiite Muslim differences, if not of the Wahhabis or Sufis. Buddhism is related to Hinduism. The Hindus have many gods. Africa has a hundred million believers in pagan gods. The ancient Greeks and Romans were polytheists, believers in many gods, some more important than others.

The classical Epicureans, about whom Karl Marx wrote his doctoral thesis, thought that the cause of our internal unsettlements was the belief in gods that punished us for ill living. They advocated a withdrawal from politics into a quiet life that deliberately shut out any such pesky concerns. Then we have the "two-truth" theory that acknowledged a truth of religion and a truth of reason. But they could contradict each other. The practical result of this thesis was a public life ruled by myths and a private order ruled by reason. Since most people could not understand most things, they were left with their myths in the public order. It kept them quiet. Both of these views were "true" in their own way.

What are we to make of this swirl around the word *religion*? We should first look at the word's meaning. Cicero held the word *religion* means to "read" again. Most writers thought it means something that binds. To be religious means to be bound to some god or thing.

Looked at as a natural virtue, religion is an aspect of justice. Justice means to render or return what is due. Thus, if I buy something, I pay for it. When I do, the transaction is complete. Justice is rendered.

But when it comes to our parents, our country, or the gods, it is less clear just what we should "return" to them. Natural religion recognizes that we cannot return to our parents all that is due to them for what they did for us. The virtue of piety simply means that aspect of justice whereby we return honor or goods or concern the best we can. In this sense, religion is based on the understanding that what we have, in many ways, was given to us, provided for us. The only real adequate response is something like thanks or gratitude.

A "natural" religion indicates what we can figure out by our own reflective reasoning about our finite situation in the world. Most people have also heard of something called "supernatural" religion. That is, some relation to the gods that is not simply what we can figure out by ourselves. It recognizes that from the human side some fundamental issues are not completely answered by philosophic or scientific reflection. This incompleteness is not necessarily a bad thing. It is the other side of our personal realization that we ourselves are not gods. We are beings who exist as what we are through no input on our part.

A "supernatural" religion, from this angle, would mean that a transcendent power did address itself to our situation. We realized that we could not figure out everything by ourselves. In this sense, it would contain a description of how to live or what reality is all about. What we heard made sense, but it was not simply a product of consistent philosophical reasoning. It seemed to presuppose that consistent philosophical reasoning was in fact going on. We actually wondered what was happening and tried to figure it out.

Thus, to be credible, a supernatural religion would have to be one that provided reasonable answers; that is, answers that made sense, that were at least feasible and consistent with the issues at hand. What the supernatural religion or revelation maintained could not contradict reason. It would have to be consistent with the problem as posed.

So in this sense, a supernatural religion does not mean some weird myth, or implausible fantasy, but a hard-headed coming together of reasonable positions that belong together in a consistent whole. The First Amendment does not "establish" such reasoning, but it does guarantee that they can be made known among us if we choose to think about them.

CHAPTER 28

ON HERESY

OFTEN, I reflect on Chesterton's 1905 book *Heretics*, a book of remarkable insight, as pertinent today as when it was written. Recently, the Heywood Hill Book Shop in Mayfair, London—a most cozy place judging from its enclosed card—sent me, at the request of my friend, "James Campbell, Esq," a hardback edition of Belloc's *The Great Heresies*. This book was originally published in 1938. The publisher of the book I was given was "The Roman Catholic Book Club, 111 Charing Cross Road, London, W.C. 2." But the book has no date listed. I am not sure if this house was the original publisher. It is definitely an old book, though ten years newer than Schall is. The book does not seem to have had a previous owner, at least no one has marked in it till now except me.

With the ever-increasing Muslim atrocities, the most famous chapter from this Belloc book is now "The Great and Enduring Heresy of Mohammed." For the same reason, its relation to Islam, Chesterton's novel *The Flying Inn* has gained considerable interest of late. Ignatius Press is publishing a new edition of it with an introduction by Robert Reilly, author of *The Closing of the Muslim Mind*.

But it is almost eerie to think today of how perceptive Belloc was and how unseeing the rest of the culture was and still is with regard to the spiritual origins of subsequent political realities and not only Islam. Mohammed was not the only "enduring" heretic—few people today will realize that Mohammed did not begin a new religion but dissented from old ones—namely, Judaism and Christianity—without which his "heresy" would be meaningless.

However, what I want to comment on here is Belloc's introduction wherein he sketches out the whole issue of heresy, what it is, why it is important. Belloc begins by noting the loss of a stable, technical meaning for the word *heresy*. It was a very precise word with a very precise meaning. It has become, indeed, fashionable to be a "heretic." There is something wrong with us if we do not have our own private "heresy." In fact, I have called Chesterton himself the real "heretic" because today "orthodoxy" itself is the most significant "dissent" from the popular relativist culture.

Modern relativism, indeed, means that everyone is a "heretic" to everyone else. As a Supreme Court justice maintains, we are each to create our own picture of the universe we live in. The universe itself has nothing to say about it. For what we hold and *what is,* it is said, have no relation to each other. In other words, we are all "diverse" now. It is blasphemous to suggest that there is something we "ought" to be, other than our own private diversity or heresy.

"Heresy is the dislocation of some complete and self-supporting scheme by the introduction of a novel denial of some essential part therein"—such is Belloc's definition. Thus, we can have "heretics" who dissent from scientific, biological, or mathematical systems of explanation. Belloc cited the amusing example of the way miracles were treated. The presupposition was that if an ancient or modern document stated some miraculous event, then *ipso facto* that statement had to be "unscientific." The philosophy of the interpreters did not allow miracles. This prior arbitrary position made any reporting of an extraordinary event to be, by definition, wrong. Needless to say, the event might be explained by another theory, but the fact that it happened was still true.

If we deny the validity of a whole system, that is not a heresy. Heresies retain much of the system from which they dissent. Belloc also used the example of the man who denied the immortality of the soul but still believed in every other Christian doctrine. This little difference might seem harmless. But if there is no personal immortality, the whole structure of Christianity logically falls apart. No salvation is possible to a completely ephemeral being whose absolute end is death.

But the major context of heresy is theological. If someone denies any truth exists in Christianity at all, he is not necessarily a heretic. But nihilism cannot last. "Human society cannot carry on without some creed." Some attention has been paid recently to young men and women who join the Islamic State precisely because they find no meaning in Western skepticism. Heresy, however, "is a subject of permanent and vital interest to mankind because it is bound up with the subject of religion, without some form of which no human society has ever endured, or can endure."

In a sense, schemes of relativism, multiculturalism, and diversity are trying to prove this position false. But the reappearance of Islam makes us wonder. "Each heresy left behind traces, and one of them, the great Mohammedan movement, remains to this day in dogmatic force and preponderant over a great fraction of territory which was once wholly ours"—that is, Christian.

Modern Europe is the result, in Belloc's view, of "heresies" that in one or other of its corners have endured, but they only have meaning in relation to that from which they dissent and its truth. It is not just on Islam or scholarship on which Belloc was up-to-date. "It is not heresy to say that reality can be reached by (scientific) experiment, by sensual perception, and deduction. It is heresy to say that reality can be attained from no other source." Benedict XVI often pointed this fact out. Science is based on quantified matter, but there are things that are not matter for which other methods are needed. The proposition that all is matter is itself not a material thing.

Belloc, in conclusion, remarked that a "modern attack" is leveled at Europe itself. It is the enemy of all the reason and revelation that went to make up Europe. He wondered what to call "the conflict between the modern anti-Christian spirit and the permanent tradition of the faith." He foretold an acute "persecution" and the triumph or defeat of Christianity itself. When this conflict happens, resulting in either defeat or return, Belloc thought the "modern spirit" of heresy and rejection could "perhaps be called anti-Christ." As I say, these sober words were written in 1938. As we look at the attacks from Islam and the control that relativism has gained on our souls, we cannot help but suspect that Belloc found the right word.

CHAPTER 29

ON FUNERALS

THE Jesuit retirement home where I have lived almost four years now usually has some seventy or eighty residents, all over seventy, all having already been blessed with many days on this green earth. We have one man over a hundred, a couple others nearing it. During the time of my residence here, some forty men, most of whom I have known, have died. The good superior of the house has officiated in over eighty funerals of men who have died here, to most of whom he has administered the last rites of the Church. So we have, as it were, a shifting population between here in Los Gatos and the cemeteries in Santa Clara and Spokane were west coast Jesuits are buried. About half the men request cremation. Even though the same rites and words are observed, the mood of a funeral is different when the dead are cremated, with the photo of the deceased beside the small box of ashes, and when the body is present in a casket.

One of my uncles on my stepmother's side was cremated. At his request, his ashes were spread on a golf course in Florida. This probably is not legal. I think one of my cousins had his ashes scattered at sea from an airplane. Another cousin of mine, a retired naval chief, went to work as a "greeter" in a funeral home in Florida. On a visit one time, he asked me if I would like a tour of the very busy funeral home (it's Florida, after all) for which he worked. I had never really had an inside view of a funeral home, even though our neighbor in Knoxville, Iowa, when I was a boy, was an undertaker. I said fine to my cousin. He showed me the caskets and the small boxes for cremated ashes.

We went in to watch a cremation furnace at work. He told me that they could not make enough cremation mechanisms, as the demand from China was so great. The whole cremation was done reverently, quickly, and carefully. He asked me if I wanted to see a body prepared for a casket. I decided against it. He laughed. Old salts often know more than old clergymen.

Why bring all this up? In *L'Osservatore Romano*, English (October 28, 2016), we find a document entitled "To Rise with Christ," from Gerard Cardinal Mueller, the Prefect of the Congregation on the Doctrine for the Faith. It is a review of the Christian idea of funerals. The essential thesis is that the traditional Catholic practice of burying the dead is still the preferred way for Christians to deal with their dead. This tradition does not mean that the increasingly common cremation is not to be permitted. The explanation for this permission lies mostly in the history of the opposition to burials based on some dogmatic issue.

At the Ash Wednesday service, we receive the ashes on our foreheads while the priest repeats the famous phrase: *"Remember man that thou art dust and to dust thou shalt return."* The fact is that we return to "dust" in various convoluted ways. If we are buried at sea, we probably end up as fish food. The Parsees in India place the bodies of the dead in large cages in which vultures devour them. India also had funeral pyres on which bodies were burned. The

Egyptians mummified bodies. In that condition, it took them much longer to return to dust. The Romans buried their dead.

Once I saw a photo of the old Masonic Cemetery in San Francisco. After the earthquake, the city expanded in that direction. The photo showed coffins being opened and bones exposed. Most cemeteries are legal entities that last for a certain number of years. If the ground ceases to be a cemetery, the remains are usually put in a common grave. All ashes and bones are mingled together. Thus, the difference between cremation and burial in terms of returning to dust is just a question of sooner or later.

Too, I recall the lovely English Cemetery in Rome, so different in mood from the Roman Campo Verano where more recent Italians buried their dead. Indeed, I have always recommended travelers to visit the cemeteries of the places they frequent to see what the local people think of death. Many old churches were surrounded by graveyards. When we compare cremation to burial, as I have suggested, we return to dust in both cases, only it takes longer if we are buried. Some skeletons can last a long time. Very few of the billions and billions of human beings who have ever died on this planet are even identifiable dust today. Our remains return to elements and soil. The world carries on.

The concern of the Congregation with funerals is, at bottom, doctrinal. Opposition to cremation was usually a reaction to some theological point. Cremation was early on said by Masons and others to be an effort to eradicate the notion of the resurrection of the body. If you returned the body to ashes, how was there anything left to resurrect? When cremation has this connotation, we still should not choose that means of dealing with the dead. Since most people no longer associate cremation with an effort to deny the resurrection's truth, the Church has granted that no real problem with cremation exists if cremation is chosen. But still, much is to be said for burial.

The history of theology, in one sense, can be seen in theories about the dead, especially the dead body. At the center of the Christian faith is the incarnation, life, death, burial, resurrection, and bodily ascension of Christ, the man-God. Even the Creed affirms that Christ "died and was buried." Obviously, if we deny that the body exists (some do) or that it really dies, or that we return as birds or other characters after death, we cannot cope with the exact meaning of Christ's resurrection. And in Christ, we find the full understanding of ourselves, of the very being we are when we look at ourselves, beings whose reality most clearly includes a body, such as it is in its particularity.

It is also clear that if we do not have a body, we are not full or complete human beings. This insight is why those who maintain that death is the end of us have a point. It is also why we have the doctrine of the immortality of the soul, why we are not complete without our bodies. The immortality of the soul is what makes the doctrine of the resurrection of the body credible and necessary. If, when we died, we simply disappeared into nothingness, it would mean that there could be no real "resurrection" of this particular person who has become a "nothing."

If the person died and became nothing, then God "recreated" the same person later on, it would mean that there was no continuity between the one who was born and lived and the one who was resurrected. The immortality of the soul, which requires its own proof, provides a reason why the person who dies and the person who is resurrected is the same person whose life is one continuous whole from death to resurrection. Otherwise, heaven and probably hell would be populated by strangers, not us.

"In burying the bodies of the dead," the Congregation affirms, "the Church confirms her faith in the resurrection of the body, and intends to show the great dignity of the human body as an integral part of the human person whose body forms part of their identity." Two things are to be noticed in this passage. First, the body is an essential part of what it means to be human. Some theory of everlasting immortality with no resurrection (the Platonic view) thus is not the teaching on this topic. Secondly, what finally matters is the whole being in its integrity of body and soul. The truth of Christian revelation we take on the authority of the witnesses. Whatever we think of this testimony, the fact remains that the "logic" of the argument is valid. The soul is not the whole human being. It is incomplete by itself, even though it is immortal. This view implies that the soul in its very reality looks to, needs, the restoration of the body. This truth is what Christian revelation is about.

The Church has seen many theories in its day on these issues. If a rite or explanation of what is going on at a burial implies or teaches something that denies these truths, then the Church cannot condone it. We can have "erroneous" ideas about the dead. One error leads to another, so thought is required of our faith. If we hold that "death is the definitive annihilation of the person," we obviously implicitly deny the truth of the teaching about the resurrection of the body. If we think that at death we witness the body as "a fusion with Mother Earth or the universe," we get rid of any separate being of what we are. Reincarnation theories would have it that death is a moment wherein some other being not ourselves comes to take our place. Others hold that matter and the body are the cause of evil, so that death "liberates" us from the body as the source of this evil. This view would make the human being a soul instead of a single being that includes matter as good.

Christ, as we recall, died and "was buried." He rose again. What is at stake is the notion of continuity between the dead and risen bodies. If there were no soul, for example, it would be pretty difficult to explain how someone who died a thousand years ago, on resurrection, could be the same person. If there were no continuity, it would mean that if Segundo died in AD 241 and rose again on the last day, there would have to be a new creation if there was nothing continuous between his death and resurrection. In other words, he would not really be the same person. That position would negate the whole point of the resurrection as we understand it. It would mean our actual lives had no meaning.

The death of Christ only required a few brief days of death, during which Christ is said to be visiting the souls waiting resurrection. His rising again meant that the same body was restored, however we want to deal the decaying issue of any dead body. So the practice of burying the dead is conceived to make clear that it is the same person who dies and who rises again, whenever that is.

Men have been perplexed by death from the beginning. The congregation mentions the various understandings of death that are incompatible with a Christian understanding of death. What it affirms, however, is that the central truth of Christianity involves the resurrection of the body. Our funeral rites are meant to teach us what this means. That is why we are solemn at death and we continue to pray for them. God did not intend death in the beginning. When it came, he sent his Son among us. Death, ultimately, as St. Paul said, has "no dominion." In our funerals, this truth is what we are to see.

CHAPTER 30

ON THE ORIGIN OF (GOOD OR BAD) ACTIONS

IN *The Rambler* for April 14, 1750, Samuel Johnson wrote, "My purpose [is] to consider the moral discipline of the mind, and to promote the increase of virtue rather than learning." Two things are clear from this passage. First, some distinction exists between virtue and learning. We can be learned without being virtuous. Learned but dissolute characters are not uncommon. We also meet, more frequently, virtuous folks who are not learned.

Secondly, the mind itself requires "moral discipline." Our very thoughts, however central to the kind of being we are, can be dangerous to us if we do not attend to their varied content. Scripture tells us that out of our inner soul come the vices (Mt 15:19). But we ought not to leave it at that. We can, on reflection, discipline even our minds. We can become habitually aware of the drift of our spontaneous thoughts. We can guide and classify them. That is, we can and should know ourselves. With good reason, we call many thoughts and feelings floating within us "temptations."

We should remember "that all action has its origin in the mind. . . . Irregular desires will produce licentious practices; what men allow themselves to wish they will soon believe, and will be at last incited to execute what they please themselves with conceiving." These are frank words, seldom heard. In a world in which limitless autonomy, plus internet and media, can be occasions of so many enticing and troubling thoughts, Johnson's eighteenth-century words strike us as doubly insightful.

Johnson goes on to explain where experience about what goes on within us is most clearly acquired. "The casuists of the Romish church, who gain, by confession, great opportunity of knowing human nature, have generally determined that what it is a crime to do, it is a crime to think." This well-turned passage also recalls Christ's admonitions about the intimate connection between thought and deed (Mt 5:28). Aquinas, in fact, held that it was well for revelation to reinforce what we could figure out by reason in this area. Hence, we are admonished not even to think of doing something evil.

Aquinas also tells us that civil law can only judge the exterior action, not directly the inner motivation or cause. But he does not deny that actions follow from what is inside, from thought and choice. Great insight into human nature occurs when we learn what people say of themselves when they are honest with themselves. Human nature includes an accurate knowledge of why and from whence things go wrong.

"No man has ever been drawn to crimes, by love or jealousy, by envy or hatred, but he can tell how easily he might at first have repelled the temptation, how readily his mind would have obeyed a call to any other object, and how weak his passion has been after some casual avocation, till he has recalled it again to his heart, and recalled the viper by too warm a fondness." What a remarkably insightful passage! Here we are again reminded that, in dealing with choices that we ought not to have made, we are at the heart of the world's great eschatological crossroad. The disordered choices we make for ourselves might well have been otherwise but for our not ruling ourselves in our thoughts.

Yet Johnson is aware that the presence of constant disordered thoughts in our souls is not as such an evil, but rather occasion for self-rule. Johnson cautions, "Pious and tender minds that are disturbed by the irruptions of wicked imaginations, against too great dejection, and too anxious alarms; for thoughts are only criminal, when they are first chosen, and then voluntarily continued." Thus, we are not to murder or steal but not even to think of doing so. The control of action begins in the guidance of thought.

What may surprise us today is the very idea that we can and ought so to control ourselves according to a standard of what is good and ordered. What is even more surprising is that this record of our souls in ruling or not ruling ourselves is precisely what we, as individual human beings, are to be judged by.

"He therefore that would govern his actions by the laws of virtue, must regulate his thoughts by those of reason," Johnson concludes. "He must keep guilt from the recesses of his heart, and remember that the pleasures of fancy, and the emotions of desire are more dangerous as they are more hidden, since they escape the awe of observation, and operate equally in every situation, without the concurrence of external opportunity." Our sins of thought remain hidden. When they become public through our action, we and the world can see them for what they are in their consequences, something we do not so easily see when they remain hidden.

CHAPTER 31

ON MULTICULTURALISM

THE modern notion that all cultures and nations can and should live together in harmony requires either a) a general agreement about the basis of virtue and truth or b) the elimination of any difference between good and evil, truth and falsity. "Multiculturalism," itself a construction of the mind, is what happens when the latter alternative is accepted, not as "true," but as "workable" or "practical." Cultures, however, are not philosophically or morally neutral. Within each are found a certain configuration of good and evil habits, laws, and customs. In earlier ages, though massive migrations and invasions occurred, it was difficult to pass from one country to another. Each culture or nation worked out the norms of how it was to live.

When large numbers of people can immigrate, legally or illegally, to other countries, they bring their cultural practices with them. People emigrate to achieve their "rights," what is "due" to them. In going to another culture, since all are equal, no one can be required to change his habits, language, religion, or customs. Everyone has a "right" to set up within the new system what he left.

The counter-assimilationist view, however, holds that if one moves to a new country, he should become a member of the new society, learn its language, manners, and customs. The reason the immigrant chose the new country or culture was because he thought it better than the one he left. This view assumes that some regimes are better than others. The purpose of states and nations is to provide a place wherein one can live in his "truth," however others might live. This view implies the power to protect one's own polity.

Many hold that all world problems are local problems. If there is a problem of poverty or tyranny in one country or area, everyone is responsible. All problems are international in scope. This position implies that we have really only one world state in which everyone is an equal citizen with equal "rights." Taxes, armies, police, laws, and customs should conform to a common idea of culture. The real enemies are those that maintain that truth, either of reason or of revelation, is possible. Peace will only come in the world when these last claims are eliminated. The established "truth" is that there is no truth.

Thus, both world and national governments must guarantee those "rights" they established. Basically, we have to rid ourselves of all institutions and ideas that maintain that transcendent truth exists. We systematically have to eliminate from the public order, in the name of "rights," all claims that are said to be rooted in a universal human "nature." Ideas holding that the family is a "natural" institution composed of man, woman, and child, that the distinction of sexes means something, that abortion is wrong, or that we ought not reconfigure man as we want, such ideas must be declared "anti-human," not to be spoken.

"The contemporary man cannot be defined by the absence of moral references," Chantel Delsol wrote in *Icarus Fallen*, "but by the rejection of an Evil and the apologetics of a Good that are taken for granted and detached from any idea of an objective truth that might give them legitimacy. It would not be right, however, to see in this attitude an inability of the mind to discover their foundations. Rather this attitude signals a refusal even to go looking for such foundations, for fear of actually discovering them. Contemporary man postulates not the emptiness of truth, but the danger of truth" (58).

And what is the "danger" of truth? It is that truth exists and measures our deeds and thoughts.

In this sense, the whole multicultural project of permitting everything, with the state as guarantor of this "right" to everything, reaches incoherence. The only kind of multiculturalism that is possible is one that recognizes a transcendent order. A multiculturalism that denies it ends up by establishing and enforcing a world order in which only what is objectively true is disallowed. The "fear" is precisely that truth does exist. The refusal to look for such truth is reminiscent of the scene in the *Gorgias* of Plato where the politician refuses to listen to argument, lest he be forced to admit its logic.

The "evil" that multiculturalism rejects is the "evil" that affirms the existence of truth. Truth is not "empty." Its fullness is rejected. Proper ways to live do hold for all cultures. This latter affirmation does not necessitate one world state or language, quite the opposite. But it does recognize that the objective distinction of good and evil, truth and falsity exists in every culture. This truth is what was at the root of the transcendent spirit that was found initially in Greek philosophy, Roman law, and Christian revelation.

CHAPTER 32

ON DETERMINISM

W E look back on our life from its conception to where we now stand. Everything seems like it "must" have happened in a definite, sequential way. Otherwise, what we are now could not have happened. Even slight deviations in this line that resulted in our existence would change or prevent what we are. We might easily conclude that we "had" to be what we are. If we did not exist, who would notice our absence or much care? That something free is also involved in explaining our existence is said to be an illusion. The world and everything in it are determined to be as they are.

Of course, if everything were "determined," we wonder, "Well, what determined it?" Was whatever determined it also itself determined? But when we think of these things, we usually are happy that events turned out the way they did. Otherwise, we could not exist. We usually think that it was not a bad deal that we came about. Yet this nagging feeling persists. This "deterministic" explanation misses something basic.

Chesterton said somewhere that if the world is determined, it makes no sense to say "thank you" to the waiter for bringing the mustard. To give thanks implies that something that did happen need not have happened. Of course, we could say that, whether we give thanks or not, we are equally determined. Looking back on either, they cannot

131

change. However adequately determinism may explain the events of the past, it seems inadequate for things now and not yet, things that come to pass because we choose them to.

Aristotle tells us that ethics has to do with those things about which we can attribute praise or blame. Ethics refers to the things that can be otherwise, things that we ourselves put into existence or change. We can either do them or not do them, do them this way or that way. It makes no sense to praise or blame someone for his deeds if what he did had to happen apart from any agency of his own. Likewise, if the murderer "had" to commit the crime, it is unjust to blame him for anything. In recent times, this same approach to what were once called "sins of the flesh" has served to take much of the guilt and most of the pleasure out of these much attended to activities. In a deterministic world, "I love you" means nothing.

If the world is determined in all its dimensions, nothing happens in it freely. Nothing can be said about it except that it happened. Just why we bother to say anything at all, if all is determined, is not clear to me. Thus, if a tight end makes a great catch, it seems useless to cheer him. Indeed, our cheer is as determined as his catch. The world is all a big illusion.

Another opposite version of determinism holds that God does absolutely everything. No real secondary causality exists. We cannot do anything. Every apparent act is really God's act. No connection is found between what we do and what happens. Things could be the opposite of what they seem to be. In this view, everything is free because God is unlimited. He can make what is into its opposite. He can make murder or adultery to be virtues, so relax. You have nothing to worry about. You just seem to have been doing something. All is God.

Now I want some laws to be determined. If I drop a glass on the floor, I want it to break. If it does not, the laws of gravity would not hold for anything. If these laws did not work, I should be floating in the air and so would the glass.

But we are a people obsessively concerned with freedom, wherever it came from. Why all this talk of determinism? Can I not make myself into what I want to be? Why am I bound to any laws that cannot be otherwise? Why can't something be right one day and wrong the next or right in this place but wrong in the next?

In the world, one agent is found that is actually free to do certain things. He cannot change the laws of gravity or morality. But he can choose not to abide by them. If he decides not to observe the laws of gravity and jumps off a cliff, they pick up his remains below. His defiance did not cause gravity to cease working.

If a human being breaks the laws of morality, consequences likewise follow. Otherwise, why break them? Such acts carry with them the mark of their origin. The world is also filled with deeds that need not have happened but did. This is the world in which praise, blame, and thanksgiving exist. It is not determined until we freely determine it.

CHAPTER 33

ON THE BEHEADING
OF CHRISTIANS

S ANDRO Magister's account of the beheading and subsequent canonization of twenty-one Egyptian Coptic
Christians in Libya, with the name of each man killed, was
heartbreaking and poignant.[8] I must confess that when I
heard the next day the remarks of Benjamin Netanyahu to
the US Congress in which he said, defiantly, that Israel is
now armed and will defend itself, I felt a touch of envy.
Our spiritual and temporal leaders can barely bring themselves to mention the terrible persecution that Christians in
too many lands now regularly undergo.

Magister recalled that these Copts had originally fled
from Iraq to Egypt, as if to warn us that there is no longer any hiding place. These Christians literally had no one
to defend them. No Christian armies exist. The words of
Christian leaders are usually: "Why does not someone
else protect us?" Appealing to the United Nations is like
"blowin' in the wind." Urban II, who called the Crusades,
is somehow looking better every time we hear of massive
killings of Christians and others by Muslims who claim,
with justification in their own minds, that they carry out

---

[8]   Sandro Magister, "Saint Milad Saber and His Twenty Companions,"
       L'espresso, http://chiesa.espresso.repubblica.it/articolo/1351000bdc4.
       html?eng=y.

134

the will of Allah. To Christians, they are terrible atrocities. To Muslims carrying out these deeds, they are acts of war and piety.

We mull over the question: "What ought to be done with these killers if ever captured?" In spite of all the talk about abolishing the death penalty, the only just answer seems to be: "Shoot them at dawn." For their acts, they show no sorrow or repentance, only a defiant courage that stops at nothing unless prevented. If freed, they will continue the killings.

Of course, if, rather than imprisoning them for a few years after a civil trial lasting three or four years, we did shoot them at dawn, much of the Muslin world would be in the streets protesting and look on them as "martyrs." Such is our world. The "separation of church and state," however wise, has left us with world leaders who cannot acknowledge either that it is Christians who are being killed or who it is that kills them. The killers, contrary to their own stated beliefs, are said to be just "terrorists," an absolutely meaningless designation. They kill for a cause that they believe in, not just to kill. They are not above using blood and gore for pragmatic purposes of winning. "Terrorism for its own sake" explains no actual group in the Muslim world.

Yet, on hearing of these executions, the prime minister and the impressive president of Egypt separately visited the families of the Coptic martyrs. They promised aid and help to build a church in their honor. These are good Muslim leaders, even though they were the ones most capable of preventing these particular killings. The Coptic Church, bless it, immediately canonized these young men—no ecclesiastical delay there.

How are we to think of these things? If we are not
enraged by them, there is probably something wrong with
us. Unlike Augustine's friend Alypius, who finally could
not resist gazing at the killings in Roman gladiatorial com-
bats, I cannot bear to watch clips of these beheadings. There
is something diabolical about them, even something diabolical about knowing they are going on and doing nothing
about them.

When anyone considers decapitation or beheading, however, he realizes that it is a method of execution with a long
history. Some friends of mine recently saw Poulenc's opera
The Dialogue of the Carmelites. In it, sixteen Carmelite
nuns were guillotined during the French Revolution. Even
today, beheading is the normal form of execution in Saudi
Arabia. St. Paul was said to have been beheaded, not to
mention John the Baptist, or Cosmas and Damien. Anne
Boleyn was beheaded in the Tower of London. The members of the White Rose group, who attempted to kill Hitler,
were decapitated. Mohammed was said to have ordered
beheadings. This gruesome method (yes, they are all gruesome) appears in Japan, China, Scandinavia, Germany, and
many parts of the world at different times in history. Evidently some of the Mexican drug cartels have found it, as
it were, "useful." The state of Utah once offered beheading
as an optional choice for condemned criminals. None ever
accepted, even though it is claimed to be the most painless
method of all—a fact Schall takes on faith!

Again, what are we to think of these beheadings of
Christians? First of all, in the mind of the killers, it does
not matter to which "branch" of Christianity one belongs.
Pope Francis talks of an "ecumenism of martyrdom."

Indeed, it does not really matter if one is a Christian. The whole culture that is not Muslim is said to be guilty and a legitimate object of war. Osama bin Laden declared war on August 23, 1996, almost twenty years ago. We thought it bravado at the time. That declaration as such has neither been revoked nor met. We did not want to notice. We called it "terrorism" not war so that we did not have to face what it really was. The idea of a religion declaring war did not fit into any categories except blaming the Christians for the Crusades, which were, as it turns out, one of the most defensive operations in history.

We mock military engagements, but it is quite clear that Europe today is largely the result of military failures, of the closing off of the eastern and southern Mediterranean spheres by Muslim conquests. These conquests turned Europe in on itself and eventually sent it around the world by sea to outflank Muslim control of North Africa and the Near East. Loss to Muslim armies and fleets at Tours, Lepanto, and Vienna would have destroyed what we know as Europe. The immigration map of Europe today, as far as I can see, largely reflects a bloodless invasion of Europe by Islam, mainly due to Europe's collective choice to stop having its own children. In other words, the rise of Islam has much to do with family life, or the lack of it, in the West. The Muslim strategy of gradually enclosing areas of Muslim law and life within Western, American, and Canadian cities, continued high birth rates in Muslim families, may well make the *jihadist* version of Islam less necessary.

But what about the thousands and thousands of Christians who have been killed? Christian peoples and even buildings are being eliminated from within the Muslim world. Will there be any place to which to flee? Are we all to suffer the fate of the Iraqi Copts who fled to Egypt, only to be slaughtered there a few decades later? What seems clear is that we have no leadership willing and able to understand the theological roots and consequent practices that claim to justify these killings.

What is left? Two of the Coptic men who were killed were brothers. Their third brother was interviewed about the killing of his brothers. He was asked what he would do if he saw a member of the Islamic State who killed his brothers? His response is mindful of what Robert Royal concluded in his earlier book about Catholic martyrs in the twentieth century. He said that they died mostly unknown, usually prayerfully, knowing there was no one to protect them.

Kamel Beshir, the third brother, replied that the ISIS tapes of the beheading of his brothers and companions did not edit out their final profession of faith in Christ before they were decapitated. We know they died martyrs. He then referred to his mother; what would she do? This is his reply: "My mother, an uneducated woman in her sixties, says she would ask (the killer) to enter her house and ask God to open his eyes because he was the reason her sons entered the kingdom of heaven."[9]

The immediate answer to the beheadings is up in the air. Some think we should pull out and let the Arabs fight it out among themselves. Others want to send in an elite force quickly to knock out ISIS. Perhaps Islam will reform itself?

[9]   Rod Dreher, "The Coptic Martyrs," *The American Conservative*, February 22, 2015, http://www.theamericanconservative.com/dreher/the-coptic-martyrs/.

Or Turkey will take over the area? Perhaps it is possible that ISIS will win, or that Iran will obtain the bomb and delivery systems. Few think that Islam will be "converted" on seeing the havoc it has caused. Israel might strike or be wiped out. ISIS may succeed in overturning the Saudi monarchy or regaining Egypt. The Europeans or Americans may wake up. Perhaps China is the solution, or Russia, both of whom have Muslim problems.

Yet, whatever the immediate policies or consequences, surely we have here the ultimate answer, spoken by an uneducated Coptic woman. Militant Islam, if it is doing nothing else, is busy populating the kingdom of God. Meanwhile, an increasingly relativist culture doubts any transcendent purpose to individual human lives, certainly not a Christian one, certainly one in which "how one lives" makes little difference. Hence, it turns its eyes in such a way that the beheadings are hardly noticed except as added dramas on the evening news. They are hardly distinguishable from the fictional violence that is shown on television every day. The fine line between reality and image is confused. Actual events like the beheading of twenty-one Egyptian Copts are merely added incidents in a busy day of imagining how we can improve the world. "Coptic martyrs of Libya, Pray for us."

CHAPTER 34

THE EPICUREAN OPTION

WHAT is known as "post-Aristotelian" political philosophy included, besides the Stoics, followers
of the Greek philosopher Epicurus and the Roman poet
Lucretius. Epicurus famously told us that pleasure is the
highest principle of being. But he also warned us to be
moderate and refined in our delights. Hedonism is a tricky
thing. Too much pleasure usually backfires into sickness
or it depresses us because it does not seem to satisfy us,
once we have it. This cautious, *ne quid nimis*, moderate
approach to things was based on a calculated hopelessness
or despair at ever finding any definite meaning either in life
or in the cosmos. It was a sign of ignorance even to try.

The world was, rather, a product of chance, just like the
scientists say. What happened in it was of necessity. Free
will is an illusion. Besides, there was this insane fear of
the gods that plagued most ordinary people. The gods were
invented by clever politicians and poets to make rule easier
by postulating mythical rewards and punishments. But a
considerable unease will come into your life if you insist on
thinking that the gods will punish or reward you for your
deeds. The gods really do not exist, but silly people insist
that they do. So how can a sensible man forget the fear of
the gods?

The only thing that makes sense is to shut off all the din and shoutings, the praisings and the blamings. The swirling passions of public life and the idiotic blatherings of academics only indicate so much hatred and stupidity. Have nothing to do with them. It is best to stop worrying about what goes on in the heavens, or in the world, or in the city. Man is not a political animal. Aristotle had it all wrong. Man's happiness, such as it is, is in himself, in shutting off what makes him uncomfortable. It is up to him to establish an inner peace for himself for the few fleeting years he has on this earth. "Withdraw from it all!" that's the only prudent way to deal with public affairs. Get as far away as possible from the shrines, the town square, the theaters, and the academies.

Here is the only wise advice: "Find yourself a quiet garden in the Rockies or in the Outback someplace." Then take care of the flowers and some chickens. Turn off all avenues of communication. They are just filled with the screams, accusations, spite, and envy of the men and women who have no clue what life is about, especially those who want to rule. We do not need to figure anything out. Nothing can be figured out anyhow. The sooner we know this the better off we are. The politicians promise everything and produce only more chaos. The only sane thing to do is to chuck it all. Enjoy what you can. Don't deceive yourself that there is any other alternative.

Sometimes, this politics of withdrawal looks rather preferable to any available alternative. The options we have to choose from are all bad. The only question is which is worse. Never has the choice between greater and lesser evils looked more pressing. And if we choose not to do anything, that only helps the worst choice. Reality won't let us alone. Fame and posterity mean nothing except more of the same idiocy. So the "Epicurean Option," for all its bleakness, can make sense to a modern weary mind. What little pleasure there is, in careful moderation, is the best we can do.

We have, however, what might loosely be called a Christian version to the "Epicurean Option." It is called the "Benedict Option." The phrase comes from the end of Alasdair MacIntyre's book *After Virtue*. The book argues that the classical understanding of virtue and vice is no longer possible in the hazy ideologies that control modern culture. In a world where the self is free to make itself into whatever it wants, a natural law or Christian notion of virtue and vice has no meaning or place to hide. But for those who still understand the deep disorders of the culture, what is their alternative but withdrawal?

The "Benedict Option" refers to the monastic tradition of St. Benedict, whose often-isolated monasteries became places that preserved what wise men in previous ages knew but almost lost to the barbarian invasions and moral corruption of late Roman civic life. It was in these centers of tradition and order that what was good in the classics and early Christian life was saved and represented anew. To these places, men finally came to learn what life was about, what men had thought and done before them. They realized that they did not have to start totally anew. The past was a storehouse of knowledge and beauty, if only it could be seen with new eyes.

The "Benedict Option" also recalls the thesis of Chesterton in his book on St. Francis. It also reminds us of what

St. Anthony did in the desert and of what St. Benedict did in establishing monasteries all over Europe after the fall of the Roman Empire. As opposed to the "Epicurean Option," the "Benedict Option" was a withdrawal into the desert or monastery away from the prevailing culture which was corrupted to its core. In the desert or behind the monastic walls, nature could be purified. All the obscene and corrupt symbols of the civic society could be forgotten. Nature could return to its normal cleanness. Men could be seen as men, women as women. The family could be restored from the gay and obscene arrangements found in the decadent city. This more virtuous and vigorous life would then be a source of transformation of the best of the classics, of Scripture, to the general populace once it realized the depths of its own corruption.

The problem with this "Benedict Option," as Jean Cardinal Daniélou once noted, was that Christianity is not intended for the few. The whole point of Christianity, as contrasted with Greek elitism, was that it was intended also for the Gentiles, for the poor and the normal, not just the chosen people. The "Benedict Option," so it is said, leaves the culture at the hands of the ideologues. It is a counsel of despair that admonishes us to flee. The counter-argument is that the main body of Christians, knowingly or unknowingly, adapt themselves to the culture so that they no longer know the difference between Christianity and the prevailing ideology.

"Social justice" then becomes but a systematic adaption to what the culture promotes. Christian ideals are "immanentizeed," as Eric Voegelin put it. Christianity comes to be the religious veneer on the kind of equality, ecology, and diversity that exists in the culture. Salvation comes to mean only that what the culture does is blessed. No sense of transcendence remains. Ways are found to "accept" or "tolerate" abortion, euthanasia, or genetic control of births in the noble name of "common good." Man is for the earth and its preservation, not the other way around as in the religious and philosophical traditions. This realism about the facts of our time again points back to the "Benedict Option" as the only thing remaining.

Hence Christians come to accept as matters of "social justice" divorce, abortion, same-sex marriage, earth warming, euthanasia, and conformity that are mandated by the culture. Social justice does not indicate a virtue of the individual but a plan to reconstruct society so that virtue will automatically emerge from social structures rather than personal choice and virtue. Christianity survives by becoming just another religion legally set apart as an instrument to pacify those who are not capable of understanding. This position, more or less, is a "baptized" version of the "Epicurean Option." The "Benedict Option" would at least preserve some living examples of an alternative to the lethal culture that is now, at least temporarily, firmly in control of most societies that once called themselves part of Christendom.

But then, into this post-Christian world, quite unexpectedly for most, there arrives in ever-greater numbers what we might call the "Muslim Option," something that ironically appeals to many prosperous but empty souls. In recent years, most of the ancient Near Eastern Christian enclaves—as it were, the "Benedict Options" of earlier centuries—that had survived hundreds and hundreds of years have been destroyed or are under threat. Their monasteries and churches even in the remotest corners of the world are destroyed, literally ground into gravel. The Epicurean and Benedict options presupposed some place to which one could escape. They depended on some political system that let them alone, or some remoteness that was outside the confines of society. Today, the cell phone can take anyone to any address on the planet. Armies no longer need tanks or heavy equipment. Pick-up trucks are often more useful and lethal. Even the remote and most renowned monasteries and churches are eradicated as alien to the new culture.

Europe and America belatedly begin to talk of fences and walls, the means that were set up to protect the medieval towns and cities from the barbarians or from the earlier armies of Mohammed. The "Muslim Option" today is peace through the voluntary or forced "conversion" of everyone to Islam as the Qur'an has mandated. No longer are people or buildings or customs contrary to the Shira allowed. While this option seems unfeasible even to such leaders as the prime minister of Egypt, it may well be the fate of a good part of Europe as it has been the fate of the Near East, North Africa, and parts of Asia. We even hear discussions of "The Islamization of America."[10] Neither Christians nor secularists can find a place to hide in this new world order in gestation.

Then, finally, there is what might be called the "Apocalyptic Option." This view would argue that what we are really seeing with the conquest of relativism, the expansion of Islam, the loss of faith of Christians, and the closedness

---

[10]   Kilpatrick, *Catholic World Report*, February 8, 2016.

of the rest of the world, China and India, is that God has seen all he needs to see about what men do with their free will in time. The projected numbers and the appointed time are near. Except for a few, men have systematically rejected the criteria of reason and revelation in and addressed to their minds. The only thing that remains to complete time's purpose is the judgment. Augustine said that as the world comes to its end, the number of believers will be fewer and fewer. The "Benedict Option," in its own way, confirms this.

To achieve the divine "plan," there was no need of establishing a perfect city on earth. Efforts to do so were an illusion and an escape from doing what was presented in his incarnation. Time has shown that men would always erect a city but not one of God. The "Apocalyptic Option" seems preposterous to most, though there was some talk about "not knowing the day or the hour" as intrinsic to its coming. Indeed, predictions of "end times" have been regular occurrences in recent centuries. Both the year 1000 and 2000 were thought by some to be the end.

But it remains of some value to us to reflect systematically on the "Epicurean, Benedict, Muslim, and Apocalyptic" options. They each have something fundamental to teach us. Each is a real option. That some options we should not choose is the essence of what it means to have free will. The Epicurean option to deny free will is just that, an option. The free will and what we decide with it remains. And this "what remains" is what we mean by history, the record of how men have chosen, of what they have or have not stood for. The "Apocalyptic Option," to be sure, is not ours to choose, though it is ours to be prepared for.

One of the things that were saved in the libraries and monasteries that have not been destroyed is the work of Plato. The central point of his "Apocalyptic Option" was judgment required of each soul on death. This was required because of all the sins and evils that went on in the world that were not punished, and all the good things not rewarded. The world is not complete until it is judged. But it is not the world that is judged but the free actions of men in the world. Many thought, perhaps, that their deeds made no transcendent difference.

The "Apocalyptic Option" remains to remind them that it makes, as it were, all the difference in the world. Epicurus sought to flee from the fear of the gods. Benedict and Anthony fled to find it. Islam claims it has it, so no space will be allowed for anything but Allah. In the end, Plato was right, the followers of Epicurus, of Benedict, of Allah, and of the "god of relativism" that replaced the gods, will all be judged by their words and by their deeds. When we put it all together, it seems only meet and just that it should be this way for those rational creatures who are, by nature, free and responsible for what they have wrought.

CHAPTER 35

ON BEING SATISFIED WITH GOD

THE advantages of having young friends scattered about is that they send you things that you are unlikely to come across in out-of-the-way places like Los Gatos. As it turns out, they are usually right. Jordan Teti is now a young lawyer up in Sacramento. Once, as an undergraduate at Harvard, he invited me to give a lecture to young Christians there. Our interview, published in their journal, *Ichthus* (Spring 2006), was entitled "On Learning to Leave College." At the time, Schall must have been worried about student princes who might think that college life and the end of human existence were interchangeable

Teti came across a new collection of the great French bishop Jacques-Benigne Bossuet's Lenten Sermons. In a roundabout way, de Tocqueville's friend, Mme. Swetchine, sent him the following passage from a Bossuet sermon:

> Lord, I know not if Thou art satisfied with me. I acknowledge that there are many reasons why Thou shouldest not be so; but, to Thy glory, I must confess that I am satisfied with Thee, and perfectly satisfied. To Thou it does not matter whether I be so or not. But, after all, it is the highest tribute that I can pay to Thee. For to say that I am satisfied with Thee is to say that Thou art my God, since nothing less than God could satisfy me.

No doubt, it would take the rest of Lent really to penetrate and appreciate this lovely passage. Bossuet died in 1704. His sermons especially, given mostly in Metz or Paris, are rightly considered classics of French literature. No doubt something of Augustine's *Confessions* is found in these words addressed to God. The Lord is the "Thou" directly spoken to. But, as it is a sermon, they are spoken before a congregation. We have the sense that the Lord is listening, that elevated language and incisive truths are not unworthy of or incompatible with our godly address. There is also something Socratic in these words. We "know what we do not know." We do not know whether the Lord is or is not "satisfied" with us, with our deeds or with our words.

Our sins—the many reasons why God might not be "satisfied" with us—are implicitly acknowledged. Their fact is not covered over before the Lord. Yet Bossuet confesses "to Thy glory," or better, "for" His glory. Confession is first to the Lord. The "glory" is a consequence of that possibility of forgiveness opened to all of us in the Redemption. Even our sins, as Augustine said, work unto the good. This fact is why we can exist with their record on our souls.

Christ came immediately "that sins may be forgiven"— nothing less. They could not be forgiven unless acknowledged. Bossuet uses the words *satisfied* and *perfectly satisfied* with himself. This is not vanity. He has done but what he was asked to do. There is something dubious and prideful with unsettled souls who refuse to accept the grace of forgiveness, as if Christ really did not have the power or intention to forgive at least "my" sins, they are so unique.

At first sight, nonetheless, Bossuet's God seems endowed with a rather cold and indifferent heart—"To Thee, it does not matter whether I be so (satisfied) or not." God is complete in His inner life whether we repent or not, whether we are satisfied or not. Indeed, God would be satisfied whether the world itself existed or not. Creation and the events in it do not change God. If they did, he could not be God.

Bossuet thus adds paradoxically that this being "satisfied" with God holds true for the great French orator even if God is not "satisfied" with him. This appears as exactly the opposite of what we might expect. If God were "unsatisfied" with us, as seems quite likely, we should not be satisfied but, if anything, in inner turmoil.

Yet Bossuet is right. This "satisfaction" with God is the highest compliment that he or any human person can pay to God. That is, he acknowledges that God is "satisfied" with him. God accepts his very existence. In so recognizing God's satisfaction with him, he praises God. To affirm that an "I" is satisfied with God is a reaffirmation that God is his God. This understanding reflects the Old Testament refrain that we are God's people and he is our God, no matter what.

Finally, Bossuet gives the reason for his own satisfaction. Nothing less than God could satisfy him. Again, this is Augustine's "Thou madest us for Thyself, O Lord, and our hearts are restless until they rest in Thee." Nothing but God can satisfy any of us. In the end, this is why we each exist. A great French bishop still has much to teach us.

CHAPTER 36

ON THE DEATH OF A
BROTHER-IN-LAW

MY brother-in-law, Jerome Vertin, died in Chesapeake, Virginia, in hospice care at about five in the morning on February 25. My sister, his wife of sixty-three years, was with him when he died. She said that he seemed most peaceful in death. I thought: "This is the reality that marriage vows prepare a couple for, the till death do us part.'" But we are Christians. Death is not a final parting, but a "passing over," as they now say. We wait our turns. Death is an end that is also a beginning.

Here in the house where I have lived for the past four years, we have seen the deaths of some thirty-five men, most of whom I have known. All were more or less the age of my brother-in-law (eighty-five). In fact, a couple of them went to the same high school with him in San Jose. The pattern described by my nephew of his father's last days is familiar. Men gradually cease to eat, lose consciousness, sleep, and die. This attentiveness is the respect we owe them. Dying men visibly remind us of ultimate things. They quietly teach us what we find difficult to imagine.

St. Ambrose gave a famous sermon at the death of his brother, Satyrus. It appears as the Second Reading in the Office for All Souls' Day. Pope Benedict cited it in his encyclical *Spe Salvi*—we are saved in hope. "Death is not a part of nature," Ambrose explained.

God did not decree death from the beginning; he prescribed it as a remedy. Human life was condemned because of sin to unremitting labor and unbearable sorrow and so began to experience the burden of wretchedness. There had to be a limit to its evils; death had to restore what life had forfeited. Without the assistance of grace, immortality is more of a burden than a blessing.

Death is both a remedy and a punishment. This passage is a warning to those scientists who want to rid us of death in this world in order to keep us alive as long as possible. With no sense of resurrection, they dicker with a this-worldly hell if they succeed. Ambrose was right. Immortality in this world without death is a "burden" that makes all other burdens seem light. Life quickly becomes the never-ending plodding on through monotonous decades with no inner-worldly or transcendent purpose.

My brother-in-law's sister is the wife of my youngest brother. They lived close by to one another for many happy years. A brother-in-law, like siblings, is just given to us from nowhere sight unseen. He is the man who discovers your sister. Jerome Vertin was a steady and familiar figure in my life. He knew things about business, investing, and finance that I had little clue about. In his free time, Jerry printed; he liked to refinish and restore old furniture to its original beauty. He and my sister had two children and adopted another. He died in Chesapeake because that is where his son, a retired navy master-chief, settled.

Over the years, I visited Jeannie and Jerry as they successively lived in Hillsdale here in California, in Portland,

Seattle, Santa Barbara, Scottsdale, Richardson, Texas, Steven's Point, Wisconsin, Medford, Oregon, San Marcos and Winchester in California, Boise, and in Chesapeake. These are mostly places in this world that I would never have seen or even heard of without their being in one or the other place for a time. Families move! During my last years at Georgetown, it was a comfort to have them fairly nearby. I could take Amtrak out of Alexandria and, in a couple of pleasant hours, reach Newport News, then the closest stop to Norfolk and Chesapeake.

My brother-in-law was always involved in his local parish, often seeing to it that things were done. Pastors came to rely on him, but he was not about to become a full-time sacristan. He seemed to know more about the rubrics of Mass than I did, which may not be saying much. He was in the insurance business, worked for many years for Sentry Insurance in Steven's Point. He was also a careful and persistent reader. He studied Scripture and philosophical issues. Several pastors relied on him to teach or explain difficult issues of Catholic thought. He was always clear and accurate. He was kind but did not suffer fools gladly.

Usually wives out-live husbands, but one must go first. One thinks of his sister now a widow. Anne Burleigh pointed out to me how frequently Scripture is concerned with widows, as if they need their own special attention, which they do. My brother-in-law was a good man. In this world, it is a good thing that a human life ends, at four-score years or whenever. Death looks to resurrection. Not to know this truth is a form of despair.

CHAPTER 37

NOTE FROM THE PRESENT UNDERGROUND

THE last lines of Dostoyevsky's *Notes from the Under-ground* are these: "We shall not know . . . what to cling to, what to love, what to hate. We are oppressed at being men—men with a real individual body and blood. We think it a disgrace and contrive to be some sort of impossible generalized man. We are still-born, and for generations past have been begotten not by living fathers. . . . Soon we shall contrive to be born from an idea." These words were written in St. Petersburg in 1864, the last year of the American Civil War.

In his 1848 *Manifesto*, Marx told us to "rise up." We had nothing to lose bur our chains. This call, however, showed considerably less insight into the future than Dostoyevsky. He told us that we would lose our fathers, and with their loss, our very being. Nietzsche, near the end of the nineteenth century, proclaimed that God was already dead in our souls. We just had not noticed. But the notion that we "shall contrive to be born from an idea" is a more haunting consideration. Without Fatherhood in God to ground the reality *that is*, we "free" ourselves to become anything but what we ought to be. The real sociological record of our time is a step-by-step, logical declination from the good

154

that is already present in the cosmos and in man. We remain free to know this good but only if we will.

Chesterton, early in the twentieth century, told us that the most horrible of human ideas was that men could be born of men, not women. Men cannot beget of men—or women of women, no matter how much they "want" to. Positive "laws" establishing "marriage" in such cases contradict reality. They place all involved at odds with the order of being.

Dostoyevsky saw it clearly. We want a "generalized man," not the particular one born of woman having been begotten by an identifiable father, with a real body and real blood. Our anonymous sperm and ova banks, our abortion factories, our random begetting, cloning, our divorces, all testify to the truth of Dostoyevsky's warning. We stand to be born of a laboratory or political "idea," not from real fathers and mothers.

We read the passage from John that tells us that the Word was made "flesh"—body and blood—to dwell among us. The Word did not appear as an "idea"; nor have any of us in our beginnings. Several famous passages in the Old Testament speak of God knowing us before we were in our mother's womb. In this sense, we were indeed in our ultimate origins "an idea" in God's creative mind. But the what-it-is-to-be-a-man is not ours to formulate or to bring forth. God's mind is not filled with abstract "ideas" but images of his own being.

What is the "underground" today? What is it that cannot be admitted; what is driven systematically from our public lives? The "underground" today is that explication of being and living that is specifically rejected by the politicized culture. The curious thing about the official deviation from the good is that it does not tolerate opposition. It cannot. Like Islam, it affirms that any view of reality that is not fully controlled by the public order is illegitimate. Elimination of freedom of religion and expression through hate language and other devices is no accident. It is the compliment that error always pays to truth.

What we must recognize is that articulated, orthodox Catholicism is today the real underground. It is what the culture recognizes that it must systematically eliminate. But this rejection follows a clear and logical path. It presupposes the Gnostic idea that laws and customs of the people are but free constructs, with no basis in reality. Our laws, however, really comprise step-by-step, logical deviations from the good that is in being, especially in human being. This good is found already present in reality.

The truth of human being is not created by man but discovered as already in him. He is not asked to become something else, but to become himself. He must choose to be what he is. He is free to be what he is created to be. He is also free to reject what he is. Such is his doom or glory.

The "modern project," as Leo Strauss called it, proposes that man becomes an object of his own science. He reconfigures himself in every way. But in the end, when he completes the declination from his own good, he will finally be in a position to see, if he will, that he was better made than he thought. We can only whisper these truths in the present underground. The order of evil mocks the order of good. It does not change its truth.

CHAPTER 38

ON WHAT IS NOT FOUND IN ENGLISH DEPARTMENTS

IN *A Literary Education and Other Essays* is found Joseph Epstein's 2011 review, "English As It's Taught," of *The Cambridge History of the American Novel.*[11] This hefty tome has seventy-one chapters with some twelve hundred pages brilliantly written, to Epstein's amusement, so that no one else but professors teaching in English departments could or would read them, and he is not sure about the professors either. English departments, as I have long suspected, are the last bastions of Marxism in the Western world. As Epstein puts it: "If one is still looking for a living relic, the fully subsidized Marxist, one is today less likely to find him in the Economics or History Department than in an English Department, where he will still be taken seriously." Ideologues can only converse with each other.

Epstein recalls those earlier happy days when a student who "majored" in English was, in effect, telling the world that he was not concerned with mundane things like business or making a living. He would follow that other world of literature that encouraged him to see things before they happened to him. "Undergraduates who decided to concentrate their education on literature were always a slightly

---

[11]   Joseph Epstein, "English As It's Taught," in *A Literary Education and Other Essays* (Edinburg, Va.: Axios, 2014). 335–40.

odd, nonconformist group. No learning was less voca-
tional; to announce a major in English was to proclaim that
one wasn't being educated with the expectation of financial
payoff. One was an English major because one was intoxi-
cated with literature—its beauty, its force, and above all its
high truth quotient." This is the literary version of Aristotle's "things worth doing for their own sake."

What is studied today is mostly governed by "race, class,
and gender" studies that make reality mostly unintelligible
and incoherent.

English departments also become pseudo-history departments that teach us how bad everything has been, especially in America. What would a stranger chancing on the
United States find out about this country? He would learn
that this country was "founded on violence and exploita-
tion, stroked through its history by every kind of preju-
dice and class domination, and populated chiefly by one or
another kind of victim, with time out only for mental sloth
and apathy brought on by the life lived in the suburbs and
characterless glut of late American capitalism. The automatic leftism behind this picture is also part of the reigning
ethos of the current-day English Department." This is not
a pretty picture.

Epstein takes *The Cambridge History of the American
Novel*, which needs a "fork-lift" to raise it up to one's
lap, with a lighthearted seriousness. How could there be
1,244 pages on such a topic that did not explain "why it is
important or even pleasurable to read novels and how it is
that some novels turn out to be vastly better than others?"
He rightly points out that if we buy the premises of multiculturalism or historicism, we have no grounds for saying

that anything is better than anything else. If Aztecs insist in sacrificing the hearts of their youth, or cannibals insist on having us for supper, who are we to impose our "beliefs" on them? The heart of Epstein's trenchant remarks deals with the issue of high and low culture. *The Cambridge History of the American Novel* "could only have come into the world after the death of the once crucial distinction between high and low culture." Yves Simon, in his *A General Theory of Authority*, considered the purpose of authority in things of the mind. Authority ought to guide us to what is worth knowing and studying. It simply ought to know that some things are better than others, closer to the truth. The function of authority is a guide that enables us to see things sooner and clearer than if left to ourselves.

Thus, Epstein remarks. "In today's universities, no one is any longer in a position to say which books are or aren't fit to teach; no one any longer has the authority to decide what is the best in American writing." And if there is no indication about what is or what is not worth reading, then any normal student will conclude that it really does not make much difference. No one has the "right" to discriminate against me if I read or write on anything. Even the rules of grammar and syntax, let alone the metaphysics behind words, disappear. We no longer affirm, with Plato, of *what is* that it is; of what is not, that it is not. Such affirmations might limit our "freedom" to deny being.

Epstein thinks that this academic dullness and ideology are responsible for students, on a large scale, deciding no longer to take the adventure of studying the literature that reflects what men ought to be, even if they do not live as they should. The dramas of our personal stories include our sins and foibles. The greatest novels abound in hints of redemption both for the noble and the ordinary, even if these hints are rejected. Students of noble literature suspect damnation is possible, even to the heroes, as well as to Miller's "salesman" or Flannery O'Connor's parsons.

This essay of Joseph Epstein, as I mentioned, is great fun. He lists several of the "dopey" words and phrases that he found in these "new-speak" chapters—*problematized, tasks himself, alterity, poetics of ineffability,* and, a word to end all words, *non-heteronormativity.* I did not have the courage to look this word up in the *Oxford Dictionary of the English Language* for fear that I might find it listed, or that it might indicate some psychic disorder that I was sure to discover in my own soul.

As practitioners of their trade, "these scholars may teach English, but they do not always write it, at least not quite." No doubt, the Cambridge publishers of this opus will be appalled at this witty review of their earnest efforts to say the last, or, at least, the latest thing about the American novel.

Epstein is no respecter of academic rankings or prestige. He tells us that Willa Cather and Theodore Dreiser are his "candidates" for the best American novelists. Today, however, in this literary field, the "barbarian" professors are "through the gates." They are, in fact, "running the joint" today. "Multiculturalism assigned an equivalence of value to the works of all cultures irrespective of the quality of those works."

No one, I think, denies that one can "learn" something even from the worst of literature. But what is the "worst" if there are no standards to distinguish "bad," "worse," "worst," let alone the "good," the "better," and the "best"? Such a question always brings us back, as Epstein has tried to show, to a consideration of whether *what it is to be human* is merely to do whatever we want to do. In a sense, great literature is also the account of what happens to us when we try to live as if there were no standards. In such living, the great novelists see in the lives that pass before them hints both of judgment and transcendence. To deny this level of being is to lock ourselves into our time and place, never to be heard of again, because all that we did, in the end, had no meaning.

As Adeimantus already implied in the second book of the *Republic*, the ancient poets seemed to tell us that, in the end, the wicked are not punished for their deeds in this world, nor are the good rewarded for their. My reading of Epstein's little essay suggests that the denizens of our English departments, and probably not them alone, have read many a curious yarn, except perhaps those in Plato. We have, in other words, come full circle. The "barbarians" are "running the joint."

CHAPTER 39

SCHALL IN OUTER SPACE

CERTAIN friends, on seeing the above title, will hint that Schall has never been anywhere else but in "outer space." Still, the topic is current with the Zuckerberg/ Hawking proposal to spend one hundred million dollars to find "outer space" life. No doubt, a few will still insist that the money would be better spent on the poor. I do not think that way. The capacity to zoom around the cosmos has already taught us many things that redound to help the poor.

This spatial enterprise does not expect to find God out there. The voyagers, were they to run into him, which isn't likely, would not recognize him. Thinking of space and life beyond our planet is not something that Zuckerberg or Hawking thought up by themselves. Space speculation goes back a long way in human literature. Man's first landing on the Moon (July 20, 1969) is now ancient history. Many distant voyages to planets and asteroids have taken place since then. We have not managed to make it outside our own solar system. That does not prevent us from thinking about it.

C. S. Lewis's space trilogy was a theological reflection on the relation between space and man's situation before God. Quite frequently, we come across fictional or quasi-scientific discussion of whether this planet has been or is being visited by other rational creatures who have figured out how to find life on other planets such as our own. These imagined creatures visiting us are mostly configured in odd shapes and sizes. Usually they betray the mark of good and evil, mostly evil, though the race of rational beings in Lewis's *Perelandra* was benign, as it had not fallen like our first parents. We earthlings caused most of the problems. All non-fallen races in the universe were already in contact with each other.

What explains this renewed drive to find life in outer space? Why is it worthwhile to spend all that cash on its uncertain accomplishment? One suspects, in the case of some scientists at least, a theological bent to show that God does not exist. Just how finding life in another planet would suggest this conclusion is not that clear. It would seem that some divine cause existed that would explain both existences.

Many hypotheses go into searching for rational life in outer space. The first is that billions of planets capable of supporting a human-type life exist in the universe. At least some of these have managed to figure out all the scientific problems of space travel and life on alien planets. Since we have already done much of this calculation with our own minds, no reason exists why others may not be ahead of us.

Moreover, they will be as curious as we are about life in other space environs. Therefore, they are searching for us by radio, spacecraft, or other means. We can probably communicate with them, when found, by using the scientific knowledge and constants that enabled them to reach us. Once we find them, assuming they do not want to plunder us or we them, we can settle down and learn what the other knows.

Many assume that our Creator intended this encounter to take place eventually. We can postulate problems like whether Christ was also to redeem the creatures on the newly found Planet X14 of *Epsilon Canis Majoris*. But we already have the same problem with the unbaptized. No theological reason rejects the possibility of life in other solar systems. Theology can also argue that we are the only rational race in the universe.

At present, we are dependent on facts. We have not found any other races, nor, as far as we know, have they found us. Whether the hundred-million-dollar investment will reveal anything more than what we already know remains to be seen. I see no harm in trying, provided that the information is provable and available to all to examine its validity. For what it is worth, I would be just as happy if they did find something as if they did not. Either conclusion, if based on ascertainable facts, would be the truth we are searching for when we undertook the efforts in the first place.

Still, one aspect of this endeavor fascinates me. It is not the wanting to meet extraterrestrial characters which would be fascinating. But that would likely produce the same problems that arise in meeting the man next door. Rather, it is the existence of knowledge itself, the kind that accurately aims a camera at a moon of Saturn. Why do the calculations, that we understand, work in this universe?

A correlation exists between knowledge derived from the universe and thought. Why is this? Neither causes itself to exist. Indeed, knowledge seems to exist before the universe itself. Were it not first there, the universe could not exist at all. Why is that?

CHAPTER 40

ON "COMPLETELY TABULATING" THE UNIVERSE

IN 1841, Fordham University in New York was re-founded from an earlier institution as the diocesan college of St. John the Baptist. Its first president was Father John McCloskey. In 1875, he became the first American-born cardinal. The ordinary at the time, Bishop John Hughes, figured that "his college would soon outdistance Georgetown and would always be the most important Catholic institution in the country—because, after all, he had not the pleasure of founding the others." Whether this prediction has come about can be disputed. But the wit of its concluding words cannot. These lines were spoken in 1941 by Father Robert I. Gannon, SJ, at the one-hundredth anniversary of the re-founding of Fordham, a few months before Pearl Harbor. (The Address is found in Gannon's *After Black Coffee*, 1946. St. John's College was renamed Fordham University in 1907.)

At this 1941 convocation, some thousand presidents, deans, professors, and guests gathered. All were decked in colorful academic robes. Gannon, who had studied at Cambridge in England, recalled his tutor having been present "at the American premier of caps and gowns at the opening (in 1876) of the Johns Hopkins University." Gannon was not enthusiastic over the "German influence on our learning institutions." He was not a fan of practical or specialized education, however much he coped with it as president of Fordham (1936–1949).

Imagine, Gannon reflected, that an earlier Fordham graduate, say, Bishop (Sylvester Horton) Rosecrans (1827–1878, first bishop of Columbus, Ohio), examined "the mental content of a modern college student (circa 1941) who had majored, let us say, in traffic problems or in hotel management; he might, in his simplicity, mistake an arts man for an apprentice." One has to know Greek philosophy and mediaeval guilds to catch the import of this episcopal "simplicity."

Education consisted more in "glancing backward" than forward. Gannon added: "To us simpler folk, this wistful glancing backward is a heartening sign. It means that more people than we realize are still aware that education, especially higher education, has a twofold function; that its aim is not only to increase knowledge, but to preserve it." We do not preserve things unless we think it important to do so. We do not seek new knowledge unless we think that something is still to be discovered. We do not do either unless we can think—period, which, I take it, was, or once was, the main purpose of higher education. Gannon stated his view succinctly: "We are fond of boasting that there has been more progress in the fifty years just passed than in the previous five hundred. But progress toward what?"

The motto of Fordham is *Sapientia et Doctrina*, which Gannon translated as "wisdom and information." He compared this motto with the *Veritas* of Harvard and the *Yahveh* of Yale. Each Harvard or Yale word is "all-embracing." But the Fordham motto stressed wisdom before information. In days before all factual arguments could seemingly be found in Google, Gannon already wondered: "How much information is it wise for one generation to know?" He was not, I think, advocating the virtues of ignorance but the need for reflective order. Few people know the technical definition of wisdom—"knowledge of conclusions through first causes." Still a few wise men are found. They say, "I believe that character, not wealth or power or position, is of supreme worth. I believe that love is the greatest thing in the world." Much current political rhetoric is precisely about how "wealth, power, and position" dominate our public life, rather than character and a love that is unselfish.

In 1941, recalling the Great War while seeing Europe already in flames, Gannon observed, "We all know that poor old Europe was sick unto death long before she decided to end it all with an overdose of modernity." With the EU's anti-Christian bias and its rapid population decline, Gannon's words are more appropriate seventy-five years after he spoke them on the Rose Hill campus.

The Fordham president did not despair. The grounds of his hope were the Liberal Arts and something he called "Christian humanism." He was naturally concerned with ultimate things, with "meriting for ourselves an incorruptible crown which shall be ours for Eternity." He called himself a "conservative," a realist for sure. "Wisdom subjects," he knew, no longer dominated any university. "Theology went overboard many years ago. Philosophy flourishes in outline form as a species of cultural history. Metaphysics has become a Roman Catholic aberration. Literature . . .

has become in practice more and more the science—or the bones—of literature"—a bleak future.

"Soon we shall have the universe completely tabulated, and no one will know what it means." The tabulation is ever more complete; what it means ever less clear. *Sapientia* and *Doctrina* seem opposed to each other. Yet universities, including Harvard, Yale, and Fordham, were founded on the premise that they belonged together.

CHAPTER 41

ON "DIVINE KNOWLEDGE"

IN an "inquiry" addressed to Thalassius (a Syrian hermit), Maximus the Confessor (d. AD 662) states, "[Christ] has designated holy Church the lampstand, over which the word of God sheds light through preaching, and illuminates with the rays of truth whoever is in the house which is the world, and fills the minds of all men with *divine knowledge.*" We read such ancient words and ask ourselves, "What is this 'divine knowledge' of which Maximus speaks?"

Logic tells us that "divine" knowledge is not the same as "human" knowledge, otherwise we could not tell the difference. "Divine knowledge" is proper only to God. To claim to have it by oneself is a claim to be God, something not unknown to our kind. It does not follow, however, that human beings have no knowledge at all. Obviously, we do. Our intellectual task is to relate "human" knowledge to "divine knowledge."

This is all fine, but how do we know anything about "divine knowledge"? The fact is that we do not know what it is unless God somehow informs us about it. Did he do this? That he did is what revelation is about.

Where does that leave us? How do we know what things are revealed to us? We cannot properly answer this question until we figure out what we can know by ourselves. In other words, our attention to "divine knowledge" depends on our "human" knowledge.

What am I implying here? Have we not figured out by reason many things which were once considered unknowable mysteries? We have indeed. Still, many fundamental issues remain baffling. So what's wrong with being "baffled"?

Well, nothing, except that we are not content with our inability to figure everything out. The world is filled with myths and theories that purport to explain everything that we cannot figure out by ourselves. At first, this inability seems like a sign of chaos. On second thought, it signifies a genuine unsettlement in our souls. We know that we ought to know what ultimately it is all about.

The next step is delicate. Is there anything that at least claims to be "divine" and not merely "human" knowledge? Aristotle said that we should strive to know all that we can know about "divine" things. The difference between gods and men is that the gods are wise, but men are but lovers and seekers after godly wisdom. Aristotle also suggested that if the gods knew what happiness was, it should be the first thing that they tell us

We wonder about such an observation. Is it possible that the gods did what Aristotle suggested? Well, yes, it is quite possible. How would we know if they did? Probably, we surmise, because their answers or instructions were addressed to our most perplexing lack of knowledge about what we are about in this world.

How do we formulate this issue? In Matthew (19:16), a young man asks, "What good deed must I do, to have eternal life?" Does not everyone ask himself this question?

Probably not in those exact terms. But even if we affirm that "My life has no ultimate meaning," we are implicitly answering the question of the young man. What does this "good," this "being saved," have to do with "divine knowledge"? If we do not know why we exist, it does not follow that no one knows. It may well be that our very "not knowing" is what opens us to accepting knowledge about ourselves. We realize that this knowledge about ourselves is properly "divine." It is something we accept as true from outside of ourselves, not something we figure out ourselves. But it does explain.

Where does that leave us? Maximus continues, "Through virtue and knowledge, [Christ] leads to the Father those who are resolved to walk by him, who is the way of righteousness, in obedience to the divine commandments."

But does this not imply that those who are not obedient to the "divine commandments," who are not virtuous and reject knowledge, are in real trouble? It does imply that.

If "divine knowledge" about ourselves is offered to us, can we refuse it? Clearly we can. So it is possible that the world contains both those who have heard of "divine knowledge" and those who have heard it but rejected it.

If this is the case, is it likely that these two "cities," those who have accepted and those who have rejected, will live calmly in peace together? Not likely. Why?

"Divine knowledge" is a knowledge about what we are, not just a sentiment. Maximus speaks of "rays of truth" in the "house that is the world." Through "virtue and knowledge," by walking in "obedience to the divine commandments"— rejection of these ways leaves us at war with one another. No reflection better explains our present public order.

CHAPTER 42

ON THE HUMAN ART
OF COOKING

IN Anne Burleigh's book *A Journey up the River*, she wrote of the human home, its formation and functioning. It circles around three objects, each of which, in every human home, has its own history. These are the bed, the table, and the desk. The crafting of each of these household objects can be among man's finest works. They represent our coming to be, our continuing in being, and our wondering what it is all about while we are here trying to find out. Cookbooks are aspects of the table, of the where we eat and dine, of what we cook, serve, and are nourished by. As the dining room table itself implies, we are nourished more than by calories when we eat together. But it is indeed the food that, as much as anything we know, puts mind and spirit together with our personhood and its opening to others.

When my parents moved off the farm into the small, northwest Iowa town of Pocahontas during the early depression, I recall that my father somehow had a job selling cookbooks. This endeavor is one of my earliest memories of a man who grew up on a nearby farm with its own varied chores. But once "in town," he had to make a living in other ways than farming to keep us kids and our mother going. I recall boxes of these cook books. For the sale of each

172

book, I suppose, he received a certain small commission. My father later worked for the Des Moines *Register and Tribune*, and then managed a *Gamble's* hardware store. He was always a good salesman and conversationalist. I think my sister still has one of these cookbooks.

In any case, Anne Burleigh has just privately published *The Family Kitchen: Through Five Generations*. She thought long about a proper title until one of her grandsons came up with the present well-chosen one. At this point, the "desk" and the "table" meet. She had kept the recipes of her mother, grandmothers, mother-in-law, sister-in-law, aunts, other relatives, and friends. They were often in hand-written notes, or sometimes personal modifications of more famous cookbook recipes as those of Julia Childs.

Even her husband, Bill Burleigh, is recorded to have become adept at making Thanksgiving stuffing and gravy, a fine art, to be sure. Her son David perfected a version of "Orange Julius," while her son-in-law, also a David, tells how to cook "Stagle Creek (Michigan) Trout." We also have Bill's cousin, Amy Oberst's "Goulasuppe." It turns out that Amy was German by birth and rearing, married to Bill's cousin. So as we become hungrier and hungrier with each dish pictured in our imagination by reading this book, we also sense a touch of the personality of those who handed on the recipes. It says much also of someone who would keep them, organize, and classify them for later generations.

Then there is "Yankee Pot Roast." Here is its explanation: "Pot roast is quintessential American food, the ultimate in soul satisfying eating. When your teenage sons and grandsons looking for what's simmering in your 'big red pot', a hefty red Creuset cast-iron Dutch oven, the answer could be a beef pot roast." That "eating" should also "satisfy" the soul is simply taken for granted. While there are diet cookbooks, the subject of "over" eating is not proper to a good cookbook, which presupposes both the virtue of temperance and the delight that things in moderation are as they are. Foods that are well selected, prepared, and cooked cannot help but satisfy us. It takes a sick mind to think that food ought to taste rotten.

Anne Burleigh had also written a life of her father, Ralph Husted. Somewhere in that book, I recall that the family, it may have been her mother's family, the Waldens, a family that goes back to early New England times, owned and operated an orchard in Indiana. In *The Family Kitchen*, we have "Gonga's Apple Cake"—also we have Gonga's "Lemon Meringue Pie," "Ham Loaf," and "Cranberry Sauce." Gonga turned out to be Anne's grandmother Walden.

The introductory comment to this apple cake is worth repeating as it gives something of the spirit of the whole book:

> This cake (Gonga's "Apple Cake") is identical to the cake that my Grandmother Walden made, except that Gonga used applesauce instead of chopped apples. She served it plain, dusted with powdered sugar, or with a caramel icing. When I was growing up, this was one of my favorite cakes, especially with caramel icing. When the leaves begin to turn in the fall, make this fine cake that fits the season. (A recipe for making the caramel is also later included.)

What is to be noted in such a passage is not just how we remember things that taste so good, but the seasonal realization that what we eat often goes along with the time of year and its moods. The "hearty" soups and foods found in this book obviously know something of winter and its snows—thus, "L. S. Ayers Chicken Velvet Soup" and "Margaret Brecourt's Meat Pie."

Somehow, having strawberries or pears, almost always green, every day of the year misses the exquisite taste of ripe pears or strawberries and the pies that go with them. And to me, the pie is the art of all culinary arts. So there are even directions on "Basic Pie Crusts." Without a good pie crust, you cannot have pie. Of course, having strawberry jam every morning is quite all right. One of my nieces makes sure that good jam and preserves are made when the season is neigh for making them. We do have here recipes for "Peach Kuchen" and "Plum Torte," both of which are best with ripe peaches and plums.

Another thing about kitchens and cooking is the smells, of coffee, of cookies baking, of chicken frying. In Belloc's *The Four Men*, he says that the one thing that babies hear in their cradles and old men hear as they die is the boiling of water in the kitchens. With modern plumbing, we do not have this experience so much, but the smells are still there. I recall my friend Dorothy Warner, herself a fine baker and cook, once telling me of the effects on a family of children, adults too, of coming home and smelling something being baked, of the almost irresistible drive that especially hungry boys have to eat what their mother has thought to bake for them. It does not much lessen, I have noted, as the boys grow older.

It is at the table, where we eat, that so much of life and its memories happen. The old monastic practice of reading at table that was still practiced in my early days in the

Order turned out to be one of the fondest memories of later life—the mispronunciations, the stories, the voices. I recall a wonderful lecture that Patrick Deneen gave at Oxford one summer on manners. He talked about the importance of the four-pronged fork in the teaching of children, especially boys, what manners might mean. They were not to gorge things down, like feeding sharks. They were to think of what they were doing, the others around them.

Leon Kass's *The Hungry Soul: Eating and the Perfection of Our Nature* is a book that teaches so well what it means to be a soul existing in a body. The two come together in eating and dining. That we enjoy what we eat is one of the most remarkable things about our relation to the world. I remember once reading a short news item from Australia. It said that the early Australian settlers had nothing to do with mussels. But when Italian immigrants made it there, they began to produce the most marvelous seafood pastas and chowders, almost as if a miracle had happened. We do have in this book "Charlotte Ann's Fish Chowder." This is Anne's sister-in-law, whose daughter said that the original recipe seems to be from a 1950s *Woman's Day Magazine*. How many good recipes are cut out from some obscure source? But among us, good things to eat exist in abundance, though we often need a cookbook to make them so. To be concerned with the poor does not mean that we feed them bad food.

I look over these recipes from the point of view of one who might eat what they propose, but not make them. Aristotle said that the gentleman should be able to cook. But like playing a musical instrument, he should not be able to cook or play the flute too well. What strikes me about this cookbook is that it is a product of a particular family's tradition.

Yet it is designed to enable almost anyone to follow directions. I confess, however, that the directions under "Apricot Brandy Pound Cake," baffle me. They read: "Beginning and ending with the flour, add the flour in thirds to the creamed mixture, alternating with the sour cream in halves, beating on low speed until blended." To klutzes like myself, this is pretty much like the directions on how to assemble a computer—unintelligible unless you can read Chinese.

This book is privately published. Though it has a copyright and is in handsome format, it is intended to be a family book, the traditions of a particular family, which as it goes forward and backward in time includes more and more kinfolk. We have two parents, four grandparents, and eight great-grandparents. We can have oodles of cousins, who have their own lines. One of our siblings may marry someone with six siblings. This family connection puts us in contact with all sorts of traditions and people within the family circle where they are known as relatives and friends. They have family reunions every so often. We thus have "Catherine McCray's Chicken Tetrazzini," "Old World Sauerkraut Supper," "Krista Edison's Kansas City Casserole," "Mexican Lasagna," "Belgian Beef Stew," "Beef & Onions Braised in Beer," "Adah Jackson's Spoon Bread," and "Julia Walden's Date Pudding." Nothing eaten or cooked, in the inspiration of this book, is off by itself without a home in which its very eating makes us glad.

In conclusion, I will resist the temptation to name other dishes that I should definitely like to try. Their very listing makes one realize the shortness and complexity of lives that good food keeps passing through their allotted years. This book even makes "Succotash" look appealing, not to mention "Wisconsin Baked Beans." I am a fan of pastries and notice that the "French Croissant" does not come up, but that is because it does not exist outside of France. This book makes us realize the intimate relation between good food, the table, the understanding, the family, and the art of cookery. Following its directions enables almost anyone, if they spend the time, capable of preparing good food for their families, not just for their bodies, but also for their souls.

The title of Kass's book, *The Hungry Soul*, is correct, as is the title of Anne Burleigh's book, *The Family Kitchen*. We are reminded, as even Kass touches on, that the title of our tradition's highest act of worship took place at a "Last Supper." To know what this "Last Supper" might be, it is necessary that we have some inkling of what a good family supper might be. It is this latter that Anne Burleigh presents for us in this marvelous cookbook that covers "five generations" of her family and looks forward to the next five generations, many of whom have already appeared and have eaten at her table.

CHAPTER 43

ON LIBRARIES

A RTEMIS Kirk was the university librarian at George-town University. "People sometimes think that librar-ies are only in the 'information business,'" she recently wrote to me. "But our true aim is to assist in the creation, critiquing, and preserving of culture from the past in order to provide for the future. As I see it, there is a vast distinc-tion between information, education, knowledge, and wis-dom. Let's hope we are fortunate enough to acquire at least a modicum of wisdom during our lives." Aquinas wrote, *Sapientis est ordinare,* "The function of the wise man is to order things." Wisdom is the knowledge of things in their causes, including the realization that the first cause must be itself uncaused.

Libraries can be distinguished into "public, private, and personal." Tell me what books, if any, are on your shelves, and I will tell you what you are. Formerly, a library meant a place of books and printed texts. Today, small electronic devices effortlessly carry the equivalent of a good-sized library. Indeed, almost all books of any note are currently also in electronic form.

Books are heavy; electronic versions are light. With a small device and a little skill, anyone can access almost any library in the world. The collected knowledge of mankind is thus at one's fingertips. But it is only "information" if I have no idea of order, of what is important, what trivial, or even what corrupting. A little knowledge is a dangerous thing. So is a lot of knowledge. But knowledge as such is good.

What difference does it make if we hear something spoken, read it in a book, or find it online in another language? When considering libraries, I think of the archbishop of Mosul in Iraq. His churches, buildings, libraries, monasteries, and flock were destroyed by ISIS in the name of Allah. How fragile libraries suddenly seem!

Barbarians were once described as those who did not know about books when they destroyed them. We have men today who know about books. That is why they destroy them. The very idea that books, even awful ones, should be kept is itself a product of a civilization that presupposes the existence of a reason from whence books originate.

A library, in Artemis Kirk's word, exists to "assist" culture. The sixteen million volumes of the Library of Congress only sit there, waiting. Books are but physical objects. As such, they "know" nothing. It took a mind to put them together. It takes a mind to decipher them. Knowledge only exists when someone actually is knowing something *that is*. Technically, neither books nor ideas exist apart from minds.

Universities, schools, governments, businesses, churches, and institutions have libraries. Libraries today are inhabited by folks looking not at books but at computer-type devices. It is, indeed, often quicker to find a text of Plato online than in a library. Libraries seem like storehouses for unread books.

Do we learn more from actually listening to Socrates question a sophist or reading the dialogue of Plato in which the same encounter is dramatized? Libraries again exist to "assist" us. Almost any decent library preserves infinitely more information than can be comprehended in any one lifetime. We are fortunate if we know even one discipline reasonably well. No one can know ten disciplines well, let alone, as Aristotle intimated, ten friends.

The most sobering, yet consoling, passage about books, and hence libraries that contain and classify them, is that found at the end of John's Gospel: "There are also many other things that Jesus did, but if these were to be described individually, I do not think the whole world would contain the books that would be written" (21:25).

The whole point of this memorable passage is that "the whole world" originates in a living Word. Our final destiny is not to read a book, even one by John or Plato, but to know, face-to-face, those who wrote them and those they wrote about. Yet the accumulated books in all the libraries, actual and destroyed, that mankind has collected in this world represent a noble enterprise, the making of man and the universe luminous.

The reason that we can be content with "a modicum of wisdom" is not that we do not wish to know all things. It is the grateful realization that we are none of us gods. No indication is found in Christianity that the wisdom that is not contained in all the unwritten books of which John speaks will not be ours.

What the libraries of this world contain is the record, or some of it, of our kind as they account for why each existing person is not content until he knows everything. His immediate problem is that, to paraphrase Plato and Augustine, he knows that he does not yet reside in the Library of the City in Speech, in the City of God itself.

CHAPTER 44

ON WHAT FOOLS LOOK
FOR IN HISTORY

CHESTERTON was born in 1874. Already in 1902, he wrote a perceptive essay on Thomas Carlyle (CW, XVIII, 21–32). He would have been twenty-eight years old, just beginning his career. But he is already Chesterton, quite articulate and quite amusing. He begins this essay by recalling Lecky's *History of Rationalism in Europe*. Chesterton is fine with this project, only he also sees the need of another book called "The History of Irrationalism in Europe." At first sight we might think that the rationalists are the good guys and the ir-rationalists the bad guys. Not so. "Rationalism is, of course, that power which makes people invent sewing machines, understand Euclid, reform vestries, pull out teeth, and number the fixed stars." It would be difficult to find a more delightful description of what reason does so that we could gain some insight into what reason is.

What about ir-rationalism? "Ir-rationalism is that other force, if possible more essential, which makes men look at sunsets, laugh at jokes, go on crusades, write poems, enter monasteries, and jump over hay-cocks." It may be "rational" not to do any of these latter things, but, if we do, we will cease, at the same time, to be fully human. Chesterton illustrates the same point with a further contrast:

"Rationalism is the beneficent attempt to make our institutions and theories fit the world we live in, as clothes fit the wearer. Ir-rationalism is the beneficent reminder that, at best, they do not fit." What is this latter quip but a reminder of what Aquinas said; namely, that we can know something about everything, but not everything about any particular thing. In any given existing thing, something is found that escapes us. The existence of anything always touches at some point both our minds that know it and the divine mind that created and keeps it in existence out of nothing.

Carlyle was famous for his histories and especially his attention to heroism. Many see in this latter interest something sinister. Chesterton did not see it this way. "His theory of the hero was that he was a man whom men followed, not because they could not help but fearing, but because they could not help from loving him." Such a reflection leads to the issue of equality and whether it means that higher intelligence or virtue are bad things, enemies of the true human good. "[Carlyle's] theory, right or wrong, was that when a man was your superior, you were acting naturally in looking up to him and therefore happy; that you were acting unnaturally in equalizing yourself with him, and were therefore unhappy." Actually, the proper subject of our unwillingness to acknowledge the true excellence that exists in another is envy, not equality. "Now Carlyle held, rightly or wrongly, that the worship of man, of the great man, was also a human function, and therefore gave pleasure to the performer of it." We are here, at bottom, broaching the question of the sin of the angels when we deny the excellence in others.

In his contrast between the Englishman Cromwell and the Frenchman Mirabeau in their different revolutions, Carlyle saw the contrast between a man of action and a man of "right." One wanted to get something done even if he could not get everything done. The other did not want anything done until first the perfect thing be done. Chesterton thought that Carlyle could understand men of action but not men of thought. "[Carlyle] never understood, and therefore persistently undervalued, the real meaning of the ideal of liberty, which is a faith in the growth and life of the human mind, vague indeed in its nature, but transcending in magnitude even our faith in our own faiths." What might this transcending our faith in our own faith mean? The vague idea of liberty that grows in our minds is transcended by the liberty in the Godhead which is a freedom that does not deny *logos* but affirms and follows its own ways which are not our ways.

Carlyle also, in Chesterton's view, introduced "into the philosophy of history one element which had been missing from it since the writing of the Old Testament—that element is something which can only be called humour in the just government of the universe." Carlyle is seen to bring back this sense of humor into the writing of history. Earlier historians were concerned with the cruelty, inconsistency, or barbarity of the neglect of labor issues as the explanation for the movements of history. "Carlyle is rather filled with a kind of almost celestial astonishment at the absurdity of neglecting it." That is to say, as I take it, that the Lord laughs at such sober thinkers who think that they can explain reality by the mechanisms of the labor theory of value.

Chesterton says somewhere that the most important thing we can know about someone is not his height, weight, work, or political views. The most important thing we must know is what he thinks of the universe. This theme comes up in Carlyle. "While Carlyle did realise that every man carries about with him his own life and atmosphere, he did not realise that other truth that every man carries about with him his own theory of the world. Each one of us is living in a separate Cosmos. The theory of life held by one man never corresponds exactly to that held by another." This view, on the surface, is not unlike that notorious thesis held by Justice Anthony Kennedy to justify all sorts of unjustifiable things.

Chesterton goes on: "The whole of a man's opinions, morals, tastes, manners, hobbies, work back eventually to some picture of existence itself, which, whether it be a paradise or a battle-field, or a school or a chaos, is not precisely the same picture, which lies at the back of any other brain." The great defect in Carlyle's histories was the failure to "realise the importance of theory and of alternative theories in human affairs." Again, the most important thing to know about another person is what he thinks the universe to be and his place in his own universe.

"The only history that is worth knowing, or worth striving to know, is the history of the human head and the human heart and of what great loves it has been enamoured: truth in the sense of absolute justice is a thing for which fools look for in history and wise men in the Day of Judgment." If it is possible to find a wiser reflection, I confess that I do not know what it is. We are not to seek absolute justice in this world. We are to realize that this is a legitimate topic, the work of a final judgment.

Chesterton's own metaphysics almost always shows through. "A man is almost always wrong when he sets about to prove the unreality and uselessness of anything: he is almost invariably right when he sets about to prove the reality and usefulness of anything." No reality exists that has no purpose, no relation to some other reality. We are not alone. We exist in an order that we seek to understand.

This is Chesterton's final assessment of Carlyle: "He was a breath of Nature turning in her sleep under the load of civilization, a stir in the very stillness of God to tell us that he was still there." How do we understand this passage? If we assume that the "he" in the last clause refers back to God, as I think it does, it means that we have become used to beholding artificial things, things like robots, computers, Toyotas, light beer, and cricket games that we have put together ourselves. Original things in their nature, including our own nature, remain. This latter is what came forth from the stillness of God. When we come to realize this, we can again feel in our very bones the original "breath" of nature, a nature we did not create, but only encountered in being *what we are.*

CHAPTER 45

ON UNITY

A NTHONY Esolen recently delineated the dangers of dogmatic diversity.[12] The other pole, unity, is equally problematic. In the recent *Telos,* Alice Ormiston dealt with Rousseau's "Tragic Desire for Unity." Why "tragedy"? Unity is a good desire that cannot be fulfilled. Rousseau was accused of loving humanity but not the odd fellow next door. Readers of Plato will understand the problem. Too much unity and too much diversity are both dangerous. Aristotle observed that unity and diversity are both good. But they need to be related in an orderly way. They should not consume each other. In political things, we call this latter effort federalism or even confederacy.

In this light, we recall Christ's reminder that he and the Father are one (Jn 10:30). Yet, in the Trinity, the Father is not the Son, the Son is not the Father, and the Spirit is neither Father nor Son. They are all "one" precisely by not being each other—one in being, diverse in person. The marriage vows speak of two in one flesh. What one is does not become what the other is. Both do not become some third substance that is neither the one nor the other. Too, we have in oriental religions the wanting to be absorbed into

---

[12]   Anthony Esolen, "My College Succumbed to the Totalitarian Diversity Cult," *Crisis*, September 26, 2016, https://www.crisismagazine. com/2016/college-succumbed-totalitarian-diversity-cult.

the all. Marx spoke of the "species man" who wants to be everything that is not himself.

A multi-party political system assured us that each difference is allowed its say in the one polity. In a two-party system, both parties belonged under the same constitution. Their differences do not imply two different polities alternating in power. One polity is united in different ways to do good things for all who belong to the same polity.

Unity is also one of the transcendental predicates—*Omne ens est unum*—every being is one being, is what it is. This unity means that the whole of a being, say, a human being, with its different "parts," is still one being. Without this extraordinary diversity of parts and functions, we could not be the kind of one being that we are. It is not really difficult to understand such things. Yet misunderstanding what unity is, to recall Rousseau, can lead us to many situations that, in the name of unity, make it impossible for us to be what we are. Rousseau famously wanted us, by obeying the same General Will, to obey only ourselves.

Over the years, I have often inquired of myself or of students, "Why is it all right to be a human being?" The import of the question is not to be missed. To be myself, as Yves Simon once remarked, I cannot be someone else. The "cost" of my being is that I am not someone or something else. Yet all these other selves are out there in the world. We seek to know them as they are.

We are social, personal, relational beings. The unity of parts that constitutes our own personal functioning, our being, the unique individual each of us is, enables us to speak of ourselves as this one person. Friendship, that exalted relationship, does not mean that I become someone else not myself.

What does it mean then? We are not called rational animals for nothing. We do not have minds just to have minds. We have minds so that what is not ourselves is not missed by any of us. Through our minds, we are potentially all things not ourselves. But we know them.

We "become" what is not ourselves after the manner of knowing, not after the manner of being. If I know that mountain, it remains what it is. I change because I know it. It is all right to be a human being because what is not ourselves still can be ours after the manner of knowing whereby we remain the unique, ir-repeatable persons we are. Yet we become what is not ourselves by knowing it.

In this sense, our personal unity includes, and is intended to include, everything that is not ourselves. Through God's gift, we are invited to know the divine Persons who are one. Thus, we are one being. We "become" all beings while remaining one being.

Most human disorder consists in some variation of not getting these relationships straight. Aristotle understood Plato's problem to consist in wanting too much unity. Or better, at least in the *Republic*, he wanted the wrong kind of unity. He absorbed the parts into the whole instead of keeping the parts to be parts in a common good that allowed them to be what they are.

The ultimate unity of things is through love and knowledge, not through one being absorbing every other being into itself. The great mystery, as Chesterton said, is that God wants what is not himself to be what it is. God's glory is manifest in what is not God.

CHAPTER 46

ON EVIL

THE "thou shalts" and "thou shalt nots" of the Ten Commandments were given to us, Chesterton thought, so that, knowing the few things we should avoid, we could enjoy the millions of other things that were quite all right to do. The Commandments were not given to cramp our style. They broaden almost infinitely the scope of what is out there for us to know and accomplish. The things we should not do, when we do them anyhow, usually, if we are honest with ourselves, turn into ashes in our mouths. They make us less than what we ought to be and know we ought to be.

Every so often, it's a good practice to take a look at evil. We live in a noticeably broken world. We need to account for it lest we be blindsided by our inattention to the real reason things do indeed go wrong. The world is likewise filled with amusing theories about why things go wrong. Most of these theories, when unpacked, avoid the real location of evil. Evil is not an illusion. When it is put into the world, it makes a difference. But nobody claims that absolutely nothing is wrong. The man who steals locks his door at night. Or, as Samuel Johnson once made the same point, if a man at an elegant dinner party solemnly tells the guests that he sees no theoretical reason for private property, the host should count the family silver at the end of the evening.

But evil is not just another "thing" either. All things are good. We might speak of evil men or angels. When we do, we do not mean that what-it-is to be this man or this angel is evil. It isn't, even when a given man or angel in fact does something terrible. Evil exists in an otherwise good agent. Why isn't this just pious double talk? It is, unless we are willing to think more carefully about it. This view will sound grandiose, but evil exists in the world of both men and angels because of a rather rash decision on the part of the Godhead. This decision invited beings that were not gods, and never would be, into the internal life of the Trinity. This "invitation" was, strictly speaking, "unnatural" both to men and angels. Whatever was "due" to them, it was not a rightful participation in God's own life. To so participate, they had to be invited and elevated in their very being.

But once this elevation happened, the tables were turned against God. That is, by his own creative choice, God could not bring into his life anyone who chose not to enter it. If he tried to bring them in against their wills, he would be contradicting both himself and the free creature he made.

So God was stuck. If any of these creatures, after discernment in their consciences, decided that they preferred themselves and their own ways, they had to be left with what they chose. Any friendship, especially the divine one, must also be chosen on both sides. God, indeed, on seeing an initial human rejection, did inaugurate a counter-plan. We call it redemption. It was premised on the fact that men still had to accept its way through the cross. Angels evidently, because of their nature, could not be given a second chance.

So what does this transcendent stuff have to do with evil? Everything, as it turns out. St. Paul tells us that the world itself "groans" because of the disorders of the free creatures, which seem to be related to each other in good and evil. The location of evil thus is found in a being that need not choose evil but does. He puts into the world, in other words, an act that lacks something that ought to be there.

Excuse me, but just how does someone go about putting a lack into his own actions? It's pretty simple, actually. We may not have it articulated into a fancy "theory," but we have ourselves and what we do as a laboratory in which to observe the point. Every choice we make could have been otherwise. This is what freedom of the will means. The Commandments suggest to us, and we know most of it by experience, that certain things ought not to be done.

As Socrates said, "It is never right to do wrong." What we do is not frivolous. Our lives mean something to God and to everyone around us. Evil means that by what we do in this world, we can choose implicitly or explicitly to reject God's invitation to participate in his eternal life. God took a chance in creating us free. To prevent this freedom from ever going wrong by its choosing, evil required God not to create us in the first place. This path was not chosen.

CHAPTER 47

A SECULAR EASTER

DURING Holy Week, Christians sometimes muse over what a contemporary secular man makes of Easter. The Latin word *saeculum*, origin of our word *secular*, meant a period of time in which everyone born in a given date was finally dead. A new *saeculum* began with new people. The word now signifies a world that does not need any revelation to clarify man's planetary or cosmic existence.

In *Beyond Good and Evil*, Nietzsche mused, "Jesus said to his Jews: 'The law was made for servants—love God as I have loved him, as his son! What have we sons of God to do with morality?'" (no. 164). This aphorism is a pretty good definition of what "secularism" has come to mean—the not being bound by any moral limitations.

From the outside, Easter seems like a jumble of outlandish bonnets, eggs, rabbits, weak Roman governors, shoutings of "crucify him," and strange "alleluias" about rising from the dead. From the inside, it purports to be a logically coherent account of a transcendent event that affects every human being.

In his *Pensées,* Pascal wrote, "Jesus Christ is an obscurity (according to what the world [*saeculum*] calls obscurity), such that historians, writing only of important matters of states, have hardly noticed Him" (no. 785). Already here, Pascal (d. 1662) provided the key to a "secular Easter." The event was not important. At the time, it made no headlines in the Jerusalem, Athens, or Roman media. It was not a political happening. A couple Roman historians later did mention a trial conducted by a Roman governor in a troublesome province of empire.

Suppose we maintain that this Jesus was not who he said that he was. We proceed to give reasons. To many, Christians appeared to be either deluded or witless to claim that this man really was the Son of God. The Muslims argue that Allah cannot suffer. So Jesus could not have been crucified. After his death, some claimed that the body was stolen. It did not rise again.

The more prevalent view today is that this Jesus was a really a nice guy, wouldn't hurt a flea. His disciples so wanted him to be alive that they imagined the whole thing. Others held that this Christ never existed. Scripture texts are unreliable. He was a fictional product of believers' imaginations. Religion is irrational anyhow. We should expect lots of outlandish claims in its name. However, we need to "respect" or "tolerate" many weird things. Too much trouble occurs when we make a big issue of them. Believers are mostly harmless. They are slavish weaklings. Nietzsche was right.

Science sometimes gets into the act. Carbon dating of the Shroud of Turin, said to have covered the dead Christ, shows apparently its origins from the same era as the Crucifixion. But this dying and rising again business? We know scientists are working on the death problem. They mainly seek to keep us alive, not jiggle some corpse back to life after it is dead. Those widely publicized near-death experiences of light and peace are interesting, no doubt. Still, like the Gospel story of Lazarus, who was said have returned to life, all those who experience near-death illuminations eventually die.

The secular Easter attentively notices the disordered lives that many Christians manifest. This same Nietzsche once remarked, in a memorable phrase, that "the last Christian died on the Cross." Christ did maintain that he came to save sinners, not the righteous that did not need much help. The one who died on the cross was, in fact, the only really sinless one among us. Nietzsche was right there.

A secular Easter implies, I suppose, that we could explain our lot in this world without the Easter account. Everything in this narrative, it is maintained, can be explained on natural grounds. Nothing really momentous happened at Golgotha or, on Easter morning, at the tomb into which the Marys gazed.

In his *Life of Johnson*, Bowell writes, "On Sunday, April 19, (1778) being Easter-day, after the solemnities . . . in St. Paul's Church, I visited him. . . . I expressed a wish to have the arguments for Christianity always in readiness, that my religious faith might be as firm and clear as any proposition whatever."

Johnson replied, "Sir, you cannot answer all objections. You have demonstration for a First Cause. . . . Yet you have against this . . . the unhappiness of human life. This, however, gives us hope for a future state of compensation, that there may be a perfect system. But of that we were not sure, till we had a positive revelation."

The secular Easter knows of "the unhappiness of human life." The Christian understands that "you cannot answer all objections." The historians thought the Easter event was unimportant. Nietzsche's Jesus rid himself of all morality. Johnson's Jesus leaves some hope. "Let us rejoice and be glad."

CHAPTER 48

ON PLAY AND SERIOUSNESS

"We must emphasize once again that play does not exclude seriousness."

—Johan Huizinga, *Homo Ludens*, 1938[13]

THE classical Latin adjectives that we see associated with the Latin noun *homo*—meaning what-it-is-to-be-a-human-being—are quite instructive. Thus, we have *homo rationale*. This phrase contains the most fundamental adjective that penetrates to the point wherein man and animal are properly distinguished. Man is indeed an animal but one with the capacity to reason, a capacity that governs all he does. In fact, as Leon Kass showed in *The Hungry Soul,* his rationality shapes his interior and exterior senses. For, in their very structures, they are ordered to his knowing ability, as is his whole being. This knowing capacity is not something added from the outside like a spare tire. It is already a power of his soul for the activity of which he is formed.

Likewise, we have *homo risibile*; that is, the being who laughs. It is a fact. We do laugh. We begin there. The

---

13   Johan Huizinga, *Homo Ludens: A Study of the Play Element in Culture* (Boston: Beacon 1950), 180.

capacity to laugh is itself an aspect of rationality. Why is this? Laughter arises from the capacity of mind to see relationships between things, or lack of them. To laugh, we have to be able to hold two or three different things together in our minds at the same time. Only an immaterial power can do this. In so doing, we realize some unexpected incongruity among things with similar sounds, spellings, or meanings. The capacity to laugh is a precious thing that lights up our days.

The term *homo faber* means literally "man the maker of things," the fabricator, the craftsman, the carpenter, the technician, the surgeon. This capacity of our minds connects us most directly with things to be made for our purposes. In this sense, our minds are proportioned to our hands through which our ideas pass into matter. We can know what things are. We can tell the difference between wood and iron. We can make things out of both. We put the stamp of our minds on the thing we want to fashion. The technology that we see all about us is the combination of mind, hand, habit, memory, and the many kinds of matter on which ideas can be impressed.

Then there is *homo ludens*, the man who plays. In some ways, this combination almost seems the best of all of them. This phrase was also the title of a famous book by the Dutch historian Johan Huizinga. It is a book that for me, at least, when once read, often comes back in my understanding of things.

There is an interesting note about the subtitle of this book—"A Study of the Play Element in Culture." The author, who knew English well, insisted that it should be "of Culture," not "in" Culture. Why did he stress this preposition? If we speak of play "in" a culture, we could simply be talking of the games people play—soccer, tennis, rugby, basketball, cricket, marbles, croquet, hockey, and many others. But if we speak of the play element "of" culture, we indicate that something of what it is to play can be found in every aspect of life, especially in those things of greater moment.

The problem, of course, is that we can confuse play and entertainment or relaxation. Aristotle had said that play is very close to contemplation, the highest of our activities. Intellectual activity occurs when we simply want to know *what is* for its own sake. When we speak of play, we speak of things of surprising profundity.

I have been struck over the years by the number of students who confided to me that they were perplexed by their athletic experience. Again and again, they were told that it was mere entertainment, or a pastime, fundamentally useless, the proverbial "waste of time." To such concerns, I never failed to recall Saint-Exupéry's "little prince" who told us that it is only the time we "waste" with our friends that counts. I found that most students could immediately see the point.

Aristotle, of course, distinguished between recreation and play. Into the mix must come, as Josef Pieper always reminds us, leisure and work. Recreation is related to work. Work and craft are good things. They require much exertion. They put needed things into the world in an artifact we can use. The human body can take only so much. It needs intervals of rest, both in the normal day (coffee break, half-time) and in the year (vacation).

Play is something else. "Playing is not 'doing' in the ordinary sense; you do not 'do' a game as you 'do' or 'go' fishing or hunting or Morris-dancing, or woodwork—you 'play' it" (37). Play is something "for its own sake." We do not "play" to do something else. We play to play, play to win.

Moreover, play is not best seen from the side of the players, though their side is fundamental. They have to be playing to play, to win. We cannot have a tennis match if our opponent is playing tennis for the exercise it gives him. We can only play tennis if we try to beat him and he tries to beat us. Otherwise, we might just as well be doing push-ups in the corner. And the drama of the "big games"—the Olympics, the World Cup, the Super Bowl, the World Series—is real.

The world does not watch these events simply for recreation. They bring forth something very basic to our existence—the final decision, the rules, the fine skills, the sense of glory and loss. Sometimes the most profound thing about the big game is not the elation of the winner but the gloom of the loser. We all realize that the number of winners is one, while the number of losers is legion.

The great thing about play, about games, is they need not exist, but do. They have existed as long as man has existed. What is so great about this aspect of play? Again, I think that Aristotle had it right, an utterly unsurprising surprising thing, for Aristotle saw so much. He had said that play was like the contemplation of *what is*, only it was not so serious.

Here, Aristotle meant that the playing of a game, as well as the beholding it, were fascinating in themselves, for their own sakes. In this sense, they are like existence.

Neither the world nor games need to exist, but do. This fact means that something is going on in the world that draws our attention simply because it is there, going on. We see it happen before our eyes. We are taken out of ourselves. We do not notice the time passing. Games are played in their own time.

Let me go back to the notion of Huzinga that play does not exclude seriousness. Chesterton said the same thing of humor. When someone criticized him for not being "serious" because he was also "funny," he explained that the opposite of funny is not serious. The opposite of funny is not funny. There is absolutely no reason that the highest things cannot be filled with joy, amusement, humor, and still be serious, still bring us to the heart of *what is*.

Play, as I have intimated, need not exist, but does. The cosmos need not exist, but it does. When we ask who beholds a game, the answer is the one who watches, the spectator. When we ask this question of the cosmos, we find that Plato and Scripture pictured the events going on in the world as the Lord watching his "playthings" carry out their destiny before him. They did not exist because God needed them for his own well-being. They existed in that same abundance that we associate with games. They need not be, yet when they go on before our gaze, they reveal to us what we are.

It is not an accident that the language of sports includes words like honor, fairness, rules, chance, cheating, skill, vanity, humility, penalty, punishment, reward, winning, losing, competition, training, and, yes, glory. Such is the stuff of our lives that we see played out before our eyes in games, as we do, in another way, in theaters and concert halls. We catch glimpses of the events of our own lives.

So there need be no contradiction between play and seriousness. The drama of our games, when we think of it, reflects the drama of our lives. This is what Aristotle meant, I think, when he said that play was like contemplation but not so serious. He did not mean games were frivolous. He meant that their very being fascinated us. We are to see in them the greater fascination with our existence, an existence that is beheld, that sees us play out lives in the serious play that decides whether we win or lose that for which we are created.

CHAPTER 49

ON FALSITY

THE "deflated" football is now part of athletic lore. The proposed solutions—"Everybody uses the same football" or "Let anyone use the amount of hot air he wants in the dang thing"—are a matter of rules to be defined ever more deftly as problems arise. The issue with New England Patriot quarterback Tom Brady was not really the appropriateness of his punishment. It was about whether the team and quarterback knew of it, to play unfairly. If they did know but refused to admit it, the affirmations that nothing was wrong were false.

On the assumption of falsity, if the truth simply was admitted, few would have minded much. Most folks would even have admired the honesty of acknowledging that "I manipulated the footballs we used." But if it was true but not admitted, we have the issue that provoked the sports world. Basically, the integrity of the game was at stake. Compliance with known rules must be expected of players, coaches, owners, referees, and equipment managers.

The "deflated" football is not the most serious aberration ever to confront the sports world. The not telling the truth when required probably is. It is a question of character. Even in a relativist world, everyone recognizes its force. Someone can tell the truth and have most people still think that he is affirming what is false. It is also possible not to tell the truth. Such a lie forces others to prove that we are not dishonest. Games depend on rules and their observance. In this sense, they are clearer than life itself about what is at issue when the rules are not observed. This clarity is the real reason we are so fascinated by them.

The word *falsity* comes from the past participle of the Latin verb *fallere*. It means to feign or to deceive. As such, it comes to mean the opposite of the truth. A "false" window is painted to look like a window. We cannot climb through it because, in fact, it is a large slab of wood. What is not true is thus what is false. The phrase "He lied to me" adds the notion that we are to speak the truth, both to ourselves and to one another. That is, what we say is what we hold in our minds to be true.

Words refer to particular things out there. That is why we have so many of them. Words are not just meaningless arrangements of letters that refer to nothing. My words are intended of their nature to lead minds to *what is*, what they refer to. Those who hear them likewise expect them to do so. Otherwise there would be absolutely no reason to listen to anyone if his words referred to nothing or, interchangeably, to anything.

Most everyone has heard the famous phrase "Truth, truth and there is no truth!" Of course, if this exclamation is true, we can have no falsity either. The notion of falsity is itself dependent on the notion that truth exists, but can be feigned. Indeed, it means that the person who says something that is "false" knows what is true. But he chooses not to admit it. This is why he is culpable for lying. This same phenomenon occurs in politics.

Falsity is not the same as error. If I make an error about something, it does not follow that I am lying. I may just be dumb or slow. I simply do not know the arguments or evidence that support the truth of something. This difference between error and lying explains why we are admonished to follow an "erroneous" conscience.

It is not because it is a good that some statement is not objectively true. It is because we are upholding the "good" that assures us that we have no conflict in our souls between what we think is objectively true, what we say of it, and how we act. And even if I do what I think is true but it is not, the evil consequences of my erroneous act still follow. I am responsible for them. This fact that evil consequences follow from evil acts done in good faith is but another proof that an objective world, not just of our own making, exists whether we like it or not.

We can affirm that something is true which is not. The fact that falsity is possible is quite revealing. It indicates what we are. Suppose that we had a world in which no falsity was possible. No lying would be possible either.

In the beginning of our tradition, the devil was called "the father of lies"—an insightful identification. In our world, falsity is the opposite of truth. We still must choose between them. In large part, the drama of our existence hinges on how we choose between truth and falsity.

CHAPTER 50

ON UNIVERSAL CITIZENSHIP

FROM high over the planet in a space capsule, all boundaries on earth disappear. It looks like one unified system below. But one better not land his craft just anywhere. He needs an adequate landing field with a reception posse that does not immediately arrest him for trespassing. The borders that separate the some two hundred countries on this planet are, geographically, oceans, rivers, mountain ranges, or surveyor's lines. When we see colorful international variety on display, say, at the Olympic parades, we become aware both of national differences and of the fact that the contestants run the same races or vault over the same bars. By winning or losing these competitions, they separate themselves from each other by a standard of excellence that transcends all the boundaries.

Why would it not be a good thing, many ask, if we discarded the political frontiers? We could all be citizens of the same world government. Why do we not just love each other no matter what? Why is there not an international citizenship that gives the "right" of passage and residence to everyone, everywhere, and at any time? Have not all men evolved equal? Are not all differences of color, race, sex, religion, and culture mere accidents? Why should we not work for this ideal of everyone being welcomed everywhere no questions asked? Why cannot we be hospitable to everyone at all times in all places? Is this openness not our natural "right"? We are now constitutionally free to believe whatever we want. Why cannot we live wherever we choose and as we choose according to our own lights? The Romans used to talk of one law, one language, and one brotherhood. Nations were still allowed to practice their own quaint habits of dress, language, and religion provided they did not conflict with the higher law. St. Paul, a Roman citizen, could travel all over the Mediterranean world speaking mainly Greek and preaching Christ crucified. Apparently, in the end, it cost him his life. Thomas More had a somewhat similar experience in the sixteenth century. More's "utopia" came to symbolize a world in which all that is not good is removed. All religions say pretty much the same things—a kind of happy getting along together. Everyone welcomes everyone else. No dogmas are unchangeable. The impediments of property arrangements, race, and class structures are all removed by universal citizenship in the world state of general well-being for all. Everything has been rendered safe for human exchange on a worldwide scale. No distinctions that would separate us remain.

Mankind is tired of all this violence. It causes wars. Wars are caused by distinctions, by differing religions, by racism, by poverty, by genderism, by property. Let everyone have access to everything. We can eliminate evil. This is the "right" of every world citizen if given his due.

Above all, no set "doctrines" exist, no "sins," except for the denial of world citizenship without restrictions. We can now control mankind's numbers, his earthly "environment," his physical and mental well-being. We can decide what we want, all of us. Marx was wrong: not "Workers of the world arise" but "Citizens of the world arise!" Nothing escapes us that we cannot explain. We are the masters of our fate now. Technology and science enable us to make and freely distribute everything to everyone.

This one earth is both our home and our stepping-stone to the cosmos and its riches that await us. The reign of the gods is over. The reign of mankind is upon us. We have nothing to fear. No commandments are found that we do not make ourselves. Our judgments decide the terms of our universal citizenship. Mankind (to coin a phrase) is within a step of reaching its destined perfection when all is given to all. Yes, we are no longer Gentiles or Jews, Romans or Greeks, barbarians or civilized, Christians or Muslims or Hindus, or Chinese. Nothing is above us. Nothing is below us. We are impatient. We have waited long enough! We are at home everywhere. Nowhere is alien to us.

I look at these claims as a reader of Augustine. He already understood most of these things in the fifth century after Christ. He thought them all mostly true but only after this life. Here, we are in a vale of tears, a broken world. We are not asked to save the world, but to save our souls in a world mostly at odds with what it means to save our souls. We are given commandments to keep, not to oppose. The only "universal citizenship" is in the City of God begun in this world following the plan of divine providence but completed in the next. The meaning of our times is straight-forward. We refuse to accept the world for which we were created. What we see about us is the universal citizenship of our collective refusal.

CHAPTER 51

"HOPE BEYOND THY SIGHT"

IN Tolkien's *Unfinished Tales*, the first story is entitled "Of Tuor and His Coming to Gandolin." Tuor is of the race of men. He speaks with Ulmo, King of the Waters, who is sending him on a mission. Tuor sees no purpose in his being sent. He has but one sword. He is fighting among beings superior to his human standing. But Ulmo replies to him, "But it is not for thy valour only that I send thee, but to bring into the world a *hope beyond thy sight* and a light that shall pierce the darkness."

In Tolkien, the one sent usually does not know how his deeds will favor others. He is to be obedient. He does not see how his works will fit into any providential plan. This plan itself includes the free actions of men, both their virtues and their vices. It is sufficient that he obey orders. They are not for himself alone. And valour? What is hope for its own sake? We do not hope in order to hope. We hope because something to hope for exists. When the bravest die, they complete their part of the mission. Their deeds, however, live on. They do not avoid death. Their hope includes it. They do not struggle just to keep alive. They sense that being alive in this world is not the whole of what reality consists.

The world, I think, does not suffer from a lack of vision. If it suffers from anything, it is from too many visions that are not true to reality. I have often wondered about the passage in John's Gospel that reads: "He who hates me hates my Father also. If I had not done among them the works which no one else did, they would not have sin; but now they have seen and hated both me and my Father" (15:23–24). No words could be stronger. The disciples are warned that they will be hated just as Christ was hated. They are not, to be sure, to return hatred for hatred. But they are not forbidden to wonder about the depths of this hatred of the divine being as it is manifested against them.

No one who hates the Son or the Father sees God. What they hate are the works "performed among them." These "works" are designed to instruct and teach men what they are. What we are from the beginning, in nature, is better for us than any alternative vision we might concoct for ourselves to explain what we are and what our individual destiny is. In this sense, we can speak of a "hope beyond our sight." The premise of Christian civilization that modern secularism, with ever increasing urgency and force, is busy ejecting from the public order is this: final human happiness is not found in this world.

All alternate visions insist that happiness is found in this world. We are our own instruments in finding or establishing it. The Son and the Father are actively "hated." In explaining and showing man what he is, it is necessary to acknowledge that what is best for us is not what we make for ourselves. It is what is given to us. In being obedient, we discover what we are, even when we do not know clearly where the obedience will ultimately take us. The "light" that "pierces the darkness" has been given to us. And we look away. We hate the light. We hate those who reflect its presence among us. They too are hated for it.

And how is this hatred manifest in our time, or perhaps in any time? It is presented in terms of "rights" and "dignity." It is utopian in character. It claims to institute social justice and equality. It systematically rejects any stamp of man's divine origin. What is said to be man's nature, his need to distinguish, as something already in being, what is good from what is evil, comes to be hated. We must rid ourselves of things in man said to be of divine origin. The state is the instrument not of a common good but of a transformation of man so that nothing of his ultimate origin or destiny can attain public profession.

In the light of such hatred, is there still valour? In one sense, that is all that there is. And why is this valorous? Because beyond our "sight," we have "hope." "Light" has pierced the "darkness." Yet darkness and hatred, in fact, are freely chosen because many, if not most, reject the work of the Father who is seen in the Son. We refuse this "light" by insisting that we have "rights" to make ourselves as we want to be, not as what is really best for us to be.

CHAPTER 52

ON PREVENTING WAR

CONCERNING shotguns, we can deal with them in two ways. We can take all the shotguns away from everybody. The only ones who have them are the ones who took them away. The question then becomes: can we trust the ones who took them away? Or we can teach everyone what a shotgun is, how, and in what circumstances to use it. The question then becomes one of personal virtue and care about accidents. We have noticed recently, in the case of Muslim attacks, that guns or bombs are really not necessary. Trucks, knives, and airplanes will do, as might poisoning the water supply. The question then is asked: do weapons have that much to do with war?

War issues of various sorts currently occur in Syria, Afghanistan, Iraq, North Korea, the Ukraine, and Iran. A dangerous spat flares between Turks and Kurds. Something is always amiss in South Sudan, Nigeria, Egypt, and Somalia. I talked to a Stanford student who was in Ruanda. Memories of that country's agonies cannot be avoided. Likewise, I read of the partition of Pakistan and India in 1947 that resulted in one of the greatest slaughters of modern times. Meanwhile, ISIS plans for worldwide jihad, while the Chinese navy seeks to control strategic sea routes. And not all is quiet on the Western front. Nations there seek to protect their own identity.

Wars are not caused by weapons. Wars may be delayed or even deterred by weapons. The occasions that begin wars, as Aristotle said, are often trivial. The causes of wars are not trivial. A major cause of war is the utopian notion that we can rid ourselves of them without creating something worse. Pacifism does not prevent wars. It more often causes them by projecting weakness.

A North Korean news agency affirmed that if nuclear war breaks out, "all will be ashes." We presume this included North Korea in the calculation. The North Korean president shrewdly seems to understand that if he gives up his nuclear weapons, he jeopardizes his whole regime. Nuclear weaponry is the one thing he has that makes him significant. Everyone knows that he can demolish the nearby capital of South Korea in a matter of minutes. He also knows that, should he do so, he would also get rid of the capital of North Korea in about the same amount of time. In the event, we would end up with a world without Koreans.

Von Clausewitz said that war is politics using other means. Matthew 24:6 reads, "You will hear of wars and rumors of wars." That observation seems empirically true, at least on a global scale over time. Aristotle also said that the end of war was peace, something political. The end of war is politics—how we choose to live.

Can wars be prevented? Hobbes thought perhaps so if we concentrate all power in the hands of a single ruler. Our mutual fear of death would result in no wars. The only trouble with this thesis is that we end up completely subject to an arbitrary state power. But if nothing is worth standing for, why bother? Heroism in battle always meant that some things are worth dying for. War attested to transcendence.

Most people will grant that some wars, however bloody, were worth fighting. Others will argue that by opting not to enter a war, things got worse for everyone. Most national boundaries have something to do with a war. Again, war is not the real problem. Wars are the result of ideas. Ideas are spiritual, therefore not nothings. Does this position mean that what is most "spiritual" is most warlike? In a sense, yes. Socrates told us that it is better to suffer evil than to cause it.

Does it follow then that if we rid ourselves of our ideas, we will abolish war? We watch the animal channel. The lions are always eating the zebras, never vice versa. And Scripture relates that the relation between Lucifer and Michael is a war. The weapons concern truth, something of the spirit.

Many colleges have courses called "peace studies." The colleges most devoted to peace are those in West Point and Annapolis.

On April 10, 1778, Boswell and Johnson spoke of war. Johnson said, "Every man thinks meanly of himself for not having been a soldier, or not having been at sea." Boswell demurred. Johnson replied, "No, Sir; were Socrates and Charles the Twelfth of Sweden both present in any company, and Socrates to say, 'Follow me, and hear a lecture on philosophy;' and Charles, laying his hand on his sword, to say, 'Follow me, and dethrone the Czar;' a man would be ashamed to follow Socrates."

Yet if we wanted to know whether the war was just or not, we best follow Socrates, himself once a soldier. Once that issue is decided, following Charles the Twelfth of Sweden makes perfect sense.

CHAPTER 53

"NOT A PHILOSOPHICAL SPECULATION"

WHEN Pope Benedict entered Westminster Cathedral for Mass during his English visit in 2010, the entrance song was the *"Tu est Petrus,"* composed by the recently knighted Scot composer Sir James MacMillan. As the ruins of many cathedrals there still attest, Scotland was once Catholic. Some clans remained so. What was the poignant line of Samuel Johnson in his *Journal of a Tour in the Hebrides*? "That man is little to be envied whose patriotism would not gain force on the plain of Marathon, and whose piety would not grow warmer among the ruins of Iona."

MacMillan was awarded the *"Catholic Herald'*s Catholic of the Year, 2015" (*CH*, December 17). He is an admirer of Benedict XVI, who also places music and beauty at the core of human life. "Beauty is the heart of our Christian faith," MacMillan wrote. "It should be paramount in our attentions as we approach the throne of all Beauty for our praises." The Church has long understood that men need beauty as much as they need bread; perhaps, in the long run, they need it more.

In *The Ratzinger Report* of 1985, we read, "Christianity is *not a philosophical speculation*; it is not a construction of our mind. Christianity is not 'our' work; it is a *Revelation*;

it is a message that has been consigned to us, and we have no right to reconstruct it as we like or choose" (97).

Popes and bishops have no more important task than to keep the essential "message" intact. "Philosophical speculations" only follow upon and aid the accurate reception of revelation and its content. Any attempt to "reconstruct" it or tone it down in the light of some fancied "construction" of the mind is itself to reject what has been "consigned" to us. It is this latter, however unpopular or alien to a given culture or era, that God wanted to be kept present in the world down the ages and to which he entrusted the Church to carry out.

Sir James MacMillan put it this way: "Many people, believers or not, have invested a lifetime in trying to water down Christianity, seeing a bland uniform secularism as some kind of inevitable next step. We do live in a plural society, but our civilization has been shaped by Judeo-Christian values and culture. Some of us will continue to celebrate this and live our life of faith as pluralists." One can hardly doubt that much of modern Protestantism and liberal Catholicism have indeed spent "lifetimes" in "watering down" the basic tenets of revelation and the reality to which they refer.

The effort to "water down" Christianity into a "bland uniform secularism" would make the Church an agent of cultural uniformity. The things that make Christianity distinct—its very revelation of Trinity and Incarnation—would be eliminated or explained away. This revelation and its distinctness, indeed, are popularly said to be the "cause" of our civil disorders. No one, then, can claim to be bound by anything but what the state allows for public peace. A universal "humanism" or "secularism" endeavors to eliminate any cause of strife. The Church thus can claim no effect outside its own walls. Religious freedom ends at the front door of any religious congregation.

The kind of "pluralism" that Sir James MacMillan follows is a more robust kind than the "multiculturalism" according to which we currently are ruled. Modern "multiculturalism," the kind that Sir James rejects, is based on skepticism. Nothing in principle is true. All religious ideas are equally wrong. None can claim truth.

In the "pluralism" of Sir James MacMillan, differences in thought and ideas are not to be hidden but to be lived openly and legally. Often, to do so, it takes considerable "courage"—itself, no doubt, an historical Scottish virtue. How often have the haunting bagpipes of the Scottish regiments conveyed this virtue in many a strange land.

The idea that peace is achieved by the forceful removal of any sign of religion, in effect, establishes "secular humanism" as a mandatory "public faith," all of this in the name of "multiculturalism." Such a concept has, as it turns out, proved as lethal and as narrow as almost any past religion. Its justification, again, is the claim that nothing is true.

With Benedict, Sir James understands that his pluralism is, rather, based on reason. It does not deny the fanaticism in some religions that needs to be met head on. But it likewise affirms that what is revealed is to be known and lived. These are the truths that he will "continue to celebrate" and stand for within the nations, beginning with his own land.

Finally, let me repeat, with Joseph Ratzinger: "Christianity is not 'our' work; it is a *Revelation*"; and with Sir James: "Beauty is the heart of our Christian faith."

CHAPTER 54

ON *COCKTAIL TIME*

IN 1958, P. G. Wodehouse published one of his "Uncle Fred Books." Bertram Wilberforce Wooster does not appear in this book, nor does Jeeves, but "Bertie's" friend "Pongo" Twistleton does, as well as a butler by the name of Albert Peasemarch. Uncle Fred is one Lord Ickenham; that is, Frederick Altamont Cornwallis Twistleton. No Yankee who knows his history can fail to notice the third element in this name. Lord Cornwallis's defeat at Yorktown in 1781 did not seem to show him down. He went on to become governor of India and later of Ireland. So Lord Ickenham seems to have come by his famous feistiness naturally. The first time we see him in action in the novel is when he niftily aims a "catapult," what we call a sling shot, at a target coming out of the Demosthenes Club across the street from the Drones' Club. With a Brazil nut as ammo, he shoots off the top hat of Sir Raymond "Beefy" Bastable, Q. C. Needless to say, Sir Raymond was not pleased.

Uncle Fred is known in other Wodehouse novels for his rather rare but exuberant visits to London or, as here, to the Eton and Harrow match. His ensuing reputation has led his wife, Lady Ickenham, to keep him down in the counties or otherwise supervised, lest further troubles occur. Pongo, "from earliest boyhood," had been aware of his uncle's "loopiness." In my view, the whole purchase price of the novel (which was actually given to me, but no matter) is repaid in full by running into this vivid word *loopiness* to describe a wayward uncle. As I have been an uncle several times over for years, on hearing it, I vowed to keep this striking word from my nephews, lest they also see its usefulness in relation to elderly family members.

But the fact is that Uncle Fred is by no means as "loopy" as we might think. His catapult shot at "Beefy's" top hat was shrewdly designed to deflate that arrogant geezer so that he would become human again. Sir Raymond lived with his half-sister Phoebe Wisdom and her somewhat useless son, one Cosmo Wisdom. Needless to say, one wonders if this name is not translated as "the wisdom of this world," much of which Cosmo seems to be lacking. The plot turns out to cast Lord Ickenham in the role of matchmaker. By the end of the book, four or five different marriages, of ardent man to beloved woman, are arranged. They could never have happened without Uncle Fred's supposed "loopiness."

However, another familiar character in the Wodehouse novels, one Sir Roderick Glossop, a psychiatrist, also appears in *Cocktail Time*. Sir Roderick is said here to be a "loony" doctor. The fine point about the distinction between "loopy" and "loony" I leave to Roget's *Thesaurus*, which useful tome in fact is cited three or four times in the novel. To wit, Sir Raymond's manner was said "not to be blithe." "Roget, asked to describe it, would have selected some term such as 'resigned' or 'nonresisting' or possibly 'down on his narrowbones' (*slang*)." Wodehouse no doubt intended to educate his unsuspecting readers by forcing them to go to Roget's or the *Oxford English Dictionary* to figure out exactly what he was talking about.

The plot of this book concerns a novel most unexpectedly written by Lord Ickenham's friend, Sir Raymond "Beefy" Bastable, Q. C., of top hat fame. Sir Raymond was a man who made much money and reputation by grilling hapless citizens caught in various crimes against the king and humanity. In the process, however, Sir Raymond lost the winning ways of his youth. He became a rather despicable character which his old schoolmate, Lord Ickenham, was determined to reform. "Beefy" lost his only love, one Barbara Crowe, now a middle aged, yet still handsome, woman. Barbara turns out to be the literary agent for Howard Saxby, the elderly publisher of *Cocktail Time*. The potential sales of this sensational novel are immensely increased when the local Anglican bishop, at the Church of St. Jude the Resilient, Eaton Square, denounced it from the pulpit as immoral.

As all Wodehouse novels are based on a most intricate plot, I shall speak no more of the events of *Cocktail Time*. It is not necessarily true that knowing a plot militates against reading it. In fact, the Greeks thought it enhanced it. But to explain the plot of Wodehouse is to rewrite it. What I do want to point out is that one needs to have a vast storehouse of information to catch the overtones and humor of any Wodehouse novel. The book of Ecclesiastes comes up several times, for instance, and the book of Revelation is referred to.

Shakespeare is often cited; even the question of whether Bacon wrote Shakespeare comes up. In the course of the novel, Sir Raymond was on an island in a lake looking for a letter presumably buried there. But it turned out that his return boat disappeared, leaving him stranded on the island.

Thus, fully clothed, he had to swim back to the mainland. People who observed this rather odd nautical event were puzzled that anyone would swim with his clothes on. His half-sister had lately thought that Sir Raymond had "lost his marbles." But Lord Ickenham, to save the dignity of Sir Raymond, pointed out that "according to Shakespeare, Julius Caesar used to swim with his clothes on." What is all right for Julius Caesar is all right for "Beefy" Bastable. I have, in fact, seen one reference to Caesar swimming while holding a letter in the air and another of his swimming across the harbor at Alexandria, during his dalliance with Cleopatra. There is a whole commercial line of clothing that Caesar swam in. So perhaps it is not so looney after all.

We find other historical events in English history, like Drake's Drum. This was apparently a snare drum. On his death, Sir Francis Drake is reported to have said that if England ever heeds him in its hour of need, he will be there with his drum. An astonishing number of crucial incidents in British history have been handed down in which people heard the drum—such as at Dunkirk or at the scuttling of the German fleet at Scapa Flow. Evidently, Drake's Drum is set to music and sung in a most vigorous manner by men who have had a bit too much to drink of the soothing brew at the local pub, "The Beetle and Wedge." "There's only one thing you have to watch out for with Albert Peasemarch, the Drake's Drum side of him. Be careful that he doesn't sing it during the wedding ceremonies"; such was the advice that Lord Ickenham gave to Phoebe Wisdom when she married the former butler, who, as it turns out, was a man of property who had served in the Home Guards with Lord Ickenham.

This novel is full of that amusement, the delight of language. Albert is thanking Lord Ickenham for his part in arranging his wedding with Phoebe Wisdom. The honorable but slightly loopy nobleman replies, "There is nothing like getting married. It's the only life, as Brigham Young and King Solomon would tell you, if they were still with us." Since between the two of them these two famous gentlemen were married more than eighty times, they should know, if anyone does. The irony is most amusing. The difference between getting married once and getting married some forty times is probably infinite, as Wodehouse no doubt intended the reader to understand.

So I want to conclude with several what? Not exactly aphorisms, but certainly insights into our human condition that we ought not to pass over lightly. The first remark concerns the press and media: 1) "If there is one thing the popular press of today is, it's nosey. It tracks down; it ferrets out." Next concerns the English weather: 2) "It was one of those perfect days which come from three to five times in an English summer." We are warned about retiring too early. After a military career, Albert Beasemarch decided to become a butler. 3) "And why did he want to buttle?" "Ennui, my dear boy, the ennui that always attacks those fellows who retire in their prime." And finally, we are reminded that some things take time. 4) "[There is] a suggestion of that Ancient Mariner, of whom the poet Coleridge wrote. Like him, he knew he had a good story to relate, and he did not intend to hurry it."

Sir Raymond "Beefy" Bastable, Q. C., at one point had wanted to enter politics. But his authorship of the lurid novel *Cocktail Time* would have not served him well with the more prudish set in England. But Lord Ickenham, loopy or not, strove to dissuade Sir Raymond from this rash act. "Why do you want a political career?" Lord Ickenham wanted to know. "Have you ever been in the House of Commons and taken a good square look at its inmates? As weird a gaggle of freaks and subhumans as was ever collected in one spot. I wouldn't mix with them for any money you could offer me." We can assume today that the House of Commons has probably passed a "hate-speech" law that would prevent even the most "nosey" press from using such descriptive words of politicians. It makes one realize, I think, how difficult it is these days to tell just who is and who is not "loopy" or "loony," however Roget might suggest their more accurate usage.

CHAPTER 55

THE NATIVITY: GOD MADE VISIBLE

I

IN the first Advent Preface for Mass, we read words reminiscent of St. Paul. We read of a "plan" that was formed "long ago." A "plan" may include, but it is not, as such, "chance." "Plans" imply a "planner." A way to "salvation" has been opened for us through this "plan." We need to understand from what it is that we need to be saved. The notion of a "plan" is an exact one. It implies intelligence and scope. What happened at the first Christmas was not a "myth." It was part of a longer story or account of which this birth in Bethlehem was a central feature. Once this birth took place, because of which it was that was born, nothing remained quite the same in this world.

Christians, to their credit, do not believe in something that never happened. The evidence for and against the factual truth of Christ's birth in "the fullness of time" has been worked over like no other fact in human history. Many seem desperate to prove it false, as if its presumed truth might directly affect them, which, of course, it would. If what the "plan" attests never happened, we need not pay much attention to it. If no compelling and solid evidence for its veracity could be found, no Christian would deny that it need not be taken seriously. Lacking evidence, Christmas at best is a pious sentiment if it is not what it said it was. It claims to be the actual birth of a human child who was, at the same time, divine. So the first thing to note about Christmas is the claim that it happened pretty much as the Gospels recount it. No Christian is fool enough to insist that what happened did not happen.

We should, to be sure, be upset if what is recounted in the Gospels is not true. It would then be like other stories, well told perhaps, about fictional characters. But the events depicted in such stories never really took place. Yet if we think of it, we probably should be much more upset if these events *did* happen as they are narrated and we did not acknowledge their truth. Then, if we refuse to accept their reality or implications, we find that we have to concoct a counter-narrative that purports to explain how they could not have happened. I do not consider these remarks to be a version of Pascal's wager that if we do not know the truth of something, we best come down on the safe or less dangerous side. The Nativity is not the offshoot of a wager about whether it happened or not.

In the first Christmas Preface we read that in the Nativity, we see "our God made visible." Through this God made visible, we are caught up in the love of "the God we cannot see." At first sight, we have two "gods" mentioned here; one we see and one we do not see. So the "plan" is complicated. One aspect of it is to teach us about God, something we could not figure out by ourselves without the need to explain this Nativity. God is indeed one, but within his single being, we have different Persons. The "God made visible," the Word, is one of these Persons. Later on in his life, the "God made visible" as a human being refers to the

"God we cannot see" as his Father. And when he comes to die on the cross, this "God made visible" tells us that he will send his Spirit, as he is called, who is not the Father or the Son. By the very fact that we attend to these differences of persons, we see the "plan" being worked out. And part of the "plan" is that we learn something of the inner life of the Godhead as we learn who the Son is.

For the sake of argument this Christmas season, let us suppose that a "plan" is manifested in Scripture. And it is basically intelligible to anyone who seeks to draw it out. Likewise, even if we can perhaps delineate a plan, that would not necessarily make it true. It would not make it untrue either. Still, human beings seek to know what they are and what they ought to be. No doubt, many sources in religion, philosophy, and culture seek to explain the human condition to us. Such views are generally worth taking a look at. It is not likely that we will find an explanation that contains absolutely no truth, however partial. On the other hand, parts or half-truths need to be seen for what they are, where they fit into a whole whereby they become fully intelligible.

II

The "plan" goes something like this. The world had a "beginning," something contemporary science seems to corroborate. God did not have a beginning. In this beginning there was God but no world. The Trinitarian life within the Godhead was complete and sufficient in itself. It did not "need" the world in order to solve its loneliness or to have something to do. Had God decided not to create cosmos and man, it would have been no defect in God. In other words, the existence of something else besides God can only be explained by an abundance and freedom in God that did not arise from some "necessity" in God. The world, in other words, and man in it, need not have existed. Their existence is not a result of some "necessity."

What follows from this consideration is that the world arises out of goodness, not evil. This source is expressed in the Genesis account when each level of being, including the whole of it all, is described as good and very good. It is possible that what is simply good might want more good to exist. This situation seems to be the case. But it is unlikely that the real cause of the existence of the physical cosmos was that God just wanted it out there to behold. Within it was an order that was related to what was most important in physical creation. This was the rational creature whose mind was open to the universe and capable of receiving intelligence.

The world was really created as an arena wherein the rational creatures, each of them in turn, could work out their destiny. Each person was to participate in the inner life of the Godhead. This participation, the reason for his creation, was more than was due to man by nature. Man is supernatural in origin, not just natural. This fact explains much about him, especially his inability to find any rest except in his ultimate Trinitarian destiny following death. The real purpose of creation was that other free beings, not gods themselves but beings with mind and will, could accept an invitation. God could not "make" anyone accept this invitation to participate in his inner life. Were he to do so, there would be no freedom, hence no love or friendship or joy. So the existing world is shot through with the contingency that comes with knowledge and free will. This need to accept or reject one's place in the plan is what makes the "plan" also a drama.

We want here to know about the Nativity of the God who is "visible." The initial invitation to participate in the offered gift of eternal life was rejected. The consequences of this rejection touch every subsequent human life. God did not prevent our actions from taking their course. What he could do was to respond to them with, as it were, a counter-plan within the original plan. This counter-plan, the one that went into effect when the first parents fell, we usually call "redemption." It means, in effect, that a way was made open to achieve the original purpose of creation. This way respected the intelligence and freedom of the rational creature. He was still free to accept or reject it. Indeed, this freedom, how he chooses, is the essential outline or biography of each existing human life.

The redemption put into effect by the "God whom we do not see" respected what was already put into being at creation. God was constrained in this sense that no one who really and freely did not want to accept his invitation to eternal life could receive it against his will. The choice to reject it, or to live according to one's own definition of what he chooses, we call, by that famous name, "hell." The notion of a heaven filled with folks who did not want to be there is obviously absurd. We are given the consequences of our freedom. The other side of this freedom is that those who accepted the invitation were to do so after the manner of the life of the "God made visible." This way included the cross. Redemption, as it actually worked itself out, included suffering. It was no accident then that the Gospels open with calls to "repent."

On examination, repentance is nothing more than the acknowledgment that God's creative and redemptive plan is in fact true. Sin is nothing more than a refusal to accept one or another element of this plan as if we could concoct something superior. It is not that we do not try to conceive some plan better than the one that is handed down to us. History is full of such proposed and lived alternatives. God has left his plan freely to be worked out in a world of competing alternatives. In one sense, the history of persecution and martyrdom, including the Crucifixion, is a record of the refusal of many of our kind to accept the plan and its purpose. We were warned that it was likely to turn out this way.

But we are here mostly concerned with the Nativity. The Incarnation emphasizes human biology. The Annunciation, Mary's "fiat," was the necessary beginning of the human life that was Christ. The Nativity is when he first becomes visible, to his parents, to a few shepherds, a bit later to a few neighbors, relatives, and people in the Temple. The birth of Christ was not a major world event. No one in Rome or Athens or even Jerusalem at the time knew anything important had happened at a manger in Bethlehem. But it did happen. The witnesses were few, but they were there. That is all we need to know. That this child so born was also divine was known by his Mother. But as his life went on, it became more and more public, more and more a line of demarcation between those who thought that the invisible God could not dwell amongst us and those who did, because they saw that the God who was visible did dwell amongst us for a time. At Christmas, this fact is what we remember. It is a fact that changes how we understand ourselves and the world itself.

CONCLUSION

BOOKS of selected essays seldom have either "conclusions" or bibliographies. These selected essays, as I mentioned in the introduction, were not put in any particular order. There are not found here major premises, minor premises, and conclusions. On the other hand, each essay comes from the same mind, the same person. They will, no doubt, reveal a certain style or consistency of purpose. Things will fit together, though any man would be a fool to think that he had everything in the right place just because he put it there. But we do set out to tell the truth. We do believe that truth is there to be told.

The purpose of the mind, as Aquinas said in the passage in the beginning of this book, is to conform itself to *what is,* to what is already there, to what it did not "make" but discovered as already there. I do not suppose a writer can do anything better than to remind his readers that the things to be known are already there in existence. They came to be without his help. He did not put them there. And the ones that he did put move around; the things of the practical intellect—the poems, the laws, the machines, the paintings, the vows—he knows by understanding their origin in mind.

The passage from Psalm 44, in a way, was the spiritual inspiration of the title to this book—*Run That by Me Again.* The Psalmist tells us that we have heard things with our own ears. These things came from our fathers. We are to listen to them again and again. "We have heard with our ears, O God, / our fathers have told us, / what deeds you performed in their days, / in the days of old" (Ps 44:1–2). Revelation is about the things told to us, things intended for us to understand and follow.

Many prefer to think man is no "big deal." Nothing could be revealed to him. He is too—how shall we put it?—"insignificant." No God would waste his time with something so paltry and so passing. But Pascal asks who is it who claims this. When we confront Pascal, we deal with a mind that sees with both mind and heart. "If we would say that man is too insignificant to deserve communion with God, we must indeed be very great to judge" (Pascal, *Pensées*, no. 511). We cannot help but be amused by the pretentiousness of the mind that tells us authoritatively what God cannot do. Because of this dubious premise, they deny that men can, if God so choses, communicate with him.

Moreover, we find learned scientists telling us that if God permits suffering and evil, he cannot be God. George Mac-Donald was a favorite of C. S. Lewis. MacDonald knew men could be inconsistent. They were not always logical. Everyone knows about the "bewilderment" that comes with evil. Most people have no trouble recognizing that some evil things do happen. As MacDonald put it, "There is a bewilderment about the very nature of evil which only He who made us capable of evil that we might be good, can comprehend." It is the same thing Pascal dealt with. We mortals "know" what God "cannot" do. Therefore, we are ourselves gods since we "know" what God cannot do. It is possible, as Augustine said, that evil is allowed that some real good might occur. If we are bewildered by this possibility, we should also be grateful for it. It is the basis of our salvation and the explanation of our own lives.

The notion that we ourselves might be involved in the "tales" that we call revelation ought not to come as a surprise to us. As Tolkien often reminds us, it is all right not to be the most significant man of our time. It is all right to be an ordinary person. We are all made for eternal life, however small or great by worldly standards. But we can agree with Bilbo Baggins that "the prophecies of the old songs turned out to be true, after a fashion." We do not always, if ever, see how our own deeds serve to fulfill the old prophecies, but, as Gandalf said, they do. He adds, "'But you [Bilbo] are only quite a little fellow in a wide world, after all.' 'Thank goodness,' said Bilbo laughing, and handed him the tobacco-jar." The only thing we need note is that passing the "tobacco-jar" is now forbidden by most laws.

And finally Plato tells us that a philosopher, just by living, will know why pleasure, money, or honor can tempt us to think that we should concentrate our lives on one or other of these things, which, in their own way, have legitimate places in our lives. But there is a "pleasure in learning the nature of things." It is something "for its own sake," as we put it in the subtitle of this collection. We have minds so that we might know *the things that are*. It should not surprise us that true things are not always the easiest things to know. But that should not deter us. When we "run" those things "by us again" that we have considered in these diverse essays, we see that the pleasure of knowing the truth follows the truth, not the pleasure.

This latter, the pleasure connected with the normal functioning of things, is a gift that goes along with the greater gift, the gift that all things that are not ourselves come back to us as things to be known. In this sense, by our being what we are—we do not want to be gods or anything else—all else is given to us. It is given because we have minds and hearts that are open to reality. We could not wholly devise this reality by ourselves. But still, if some time we ran it by us again, we might begin to see the truth of things, the truth of *what is*.

BIBLIOGRAPHY

THOUGH throughout this text certain books have been mentioned, collections of essays really do not need bibliographies. When I consider all the things that I have never read, I think it a bit pretentious to suggest some books that I have read. Yet if the chance reader of this book would like some suggestions of things to read that he might otherwise never have come across, I will cite below ten books that if read, will certainly suggest that things make much more sense than one might otherwise have suspected. I am in the habit of ending previous books with book-lists. Indeed, my *Another Sort of Learning* is a book about books to list and read.

In the list below, I have not hesitated to include what Peter Redpath called "difficult" books. Indeed, Redpath wrote a book called precisely *How to Read a Difficult Book.* But we can "run by" difficult books again. The important thing is the truth and where to find it—sometimes in difficult books, sometimes in selected short essays. Samuel Johnson was not wrong when he told Boswell that the best thing you could do for a young lad was "to teach him how to read." Once he is free to read, he can seek the truth of things. Still, as a famous passage goes, it is only the truth that "will set us free."

Ten Books

1. Augustine, *Confessions.*

2. *Josef Pieper—an Anthology.*

3. E. F. Schumacher, *A Guide for the Perplexed.*

4. John von Heyking, *The Form of Politics: Plato and Aristotle on Friendship.*

5. Robert Sokolowski, *The Phenomenology of the Human Person.*

6. G. K. Chesterton, *Orthodoxy.*

7. Robert Royal, *A Deeper Vision: The Catholic Intellectual Tradition in the Twentieth Century.*

8. Jennifer Robak Morse, *Love and Economics.*

9. Hilaire Belloc, *Selected Essays* (Penguin 1958).

10. Etienne Gilson, *The Unity of Philosophical Experience.*